BOOK 3
Junior Cycle SPHE

MY
life

Stephanie Mangan

FOLENS
Wellbeing

FREE eBook
on purchase of this textbook*

Simply...

1 Scratch the foil below to reveal your unique licence code.

2 Visit **folensonline.ie/redeem**

3 Follow the simple steps outlined there.

*Teachers – please go to FolensOnline.ie

FOLENS

First published in 2018 by Folens Publishers

Hibernian Industrial Estate, Greenhills Road, Tallaght, Dublin 24

© Stephanie Mangan 2018

ISBN 978-1-78090-755-0

To the best of the publisher's knowledge, information in this book was correct at the time of going to press. No responsibility can be taken for any errors.

The FOLENS company name and associated logos are trademarks of Folens Publishers, registered in Ireland and other countries.

Acknowledgements

The author and publisher would like to thank iStock and Shutterstock for permission to reproduce photographs.

The publisher has made every effort to contact all copyright holders but if any have been overlooked, we will be pleased to make any necessary arrangements.

Any links or references to external websites should not be construed as an endorsement by Folens of the content or views of these websites.

Contents

Preface

You have made it to Third Year – welcome to *My Life 3*. This year more than ever, SPHE will be an important subject for you. Not only will it be a welcome escape from note-taking, studying and practising exam questions, but you will also learn about useful and important topics, such as:

* Identifying personal goals and ways in which they might be achieved

* Understanding how diet, physical activity, sleep and relaxation contribute to self-confidence, self-esteem and wellbeing

* Dealing with relationship difficulties experienced by young people

* Further developing your coping skills for managing life's challenges

* Practising some relaxation techniques that can help you deal with stress in Third Year

Like last year, your teacher may ask you to complete a classroom-based assessment in SPHE for your Junior Cycle Profile of Achievement. There is no final exam in SPHE.

You will inevitably experience some stress this year as you approach your first big exam, but it is important to remember that stress is not a bad thing if you deal with it in a positive way. I hope that the skills you learn in *My Life 3* will help you to do so and will help to make this year an enjoyable one.

Stephanie Mangan

Stephanie Mangan

Introduction

There are lots of activities in this book that may involve working together or working on your own. There might not always be time to do every activity, so your teacher will decide which activities your class will do. Below are the activity symbols that you will see in the book with an explanation of what each symbol means.

Wellbeing indicators

The Wellbeing indicators are Active, Responsible, Connected, Resilient, Respected and Aware. You will see these symbols at the beginning of each lesson to denote which Wellbeing indicators are developed in that lesson.

Learning outcomes

Learning outcomes are stated at the beginning of each strand to give you a clear indication of what you are expected to learn in that strand.

Learning intentions

Learning intentions are clearly visible at the beginning of each lesson. They state what you should know, understand or be able to do by the end of that lesson.

Key words

You will notice key words at the beginning of each lesson and definitions in key word boxes throughout the book.

Warm-up activities

Each lesson starts with an optional warm-up activity.

Individual work

When you see this symbol, you have to do the work on your own.

Pair work

This means that you work together as a pair. Your teacher will assign you a partner.

Group work

This symbol indicates that this activity should be done in groups. Your teacher will divide you into groups.

Class discussion

This means that the class should discuss a particular topic. Your teacher will lead the discussion.

Class activity

This means that the class should work together. Your teacher will give roles or jobs to individuals or groups.

Numeracy

This symbol means that you will have an opportunity to use and improve your numeracy skills.

Lesson link

You will see the lesson link symbol where a topic links with another lesson in *My Life*.

Subject link

You will see this symbol when a topic relates to another Junior Cycle subject.

Go online

This symbol indicates that you should find further information on the internet at home or at school with your teacher's or parent's permission.

FolensOnline 'play'

There are many digital resources for *My Life* on FolensOnline. These include:

* Animations
* Videos
* PowerPoint presentations
* Links to other websites

Activities in this book are often based on these digital resources.

Positive message

You will see a positive message exercise at the end of every lesson. This activity helps to improve your problem-solving and coping skills by using information that you learned in that lesson.

Rapid recap

At the end of each lesson, the rapid recap encourages you to revise what you have learned and to focus on what you need to find out. You can show this to your parents to let them know what you are learning about in SPHE.

Assessment idea

Your teacher will tell you whether you are to do this assessment. He or she will give you guidelines, assign groups and give a submission date.

Homework

This is the homework for you to complete at home relating to each lesson.

Personal learning journal

Your personal learning journal is a private record that you keep at home. You are encouraged to write in it throughout the year to reflect on what you have learned in SPHE.

Strand review

SPHE offers opportunities to support all eight key skills of the Junior Cycle curriculum. A strand review section appears at the end of each strand and is based on these key skills. This can help you to reflect on what you have learned, identify strengths and select areas for improvement.

Who am I?

This strand focuses on developing self-awareness and building self-esteem.

Strand learning outcomes

- Participate in informed discussions about the impact of physical, emotional, psychological and social development in adolescence

- Recognise how sexuality and gender identity are part of what it means to be human and have biological, psychological, cultural, social and spiritual dimensions

- Identify short-, medium- and long-term personal goals and ways in which they might be achieved

- Apply decision-making skills in a variety of situations

- Appreciate the importance of respectful and inclusive behaviour in promoting a safe environment free from bias and discrimination

1. Being me

At the end of this lesson, you will:

 Have reflected on your maturity

 Appreciate how the opportunities that you have in school and the community contribute to your development

 Have examined how gender can have an impact on your education

Key words
abc
Opportunity

Aware
Responsible

■ Opportunity ■

Your teacher will pick any letter from the alphabet. Using that letter, tell the class three things about your summer holidays. For example, if your teacher picks the letter S, you could say, 'I *swam* in the Irish Sea when I stayed with my cousins in Dublin; *sixteen* is the age I turned in July and I had a party; *seventy-five euro* is how much money I earned babysitting for my sister.'

Most young people want to do well in school so that they can get a good job and progress in life. Teenagers in Ireland today have many opportunities through school or the community, such as school trips, sports teams, drama clubs, scouts groups, music classes, and so on. If you are doing Transition Year next year, you will have many additional opportunities, such as work experience or learning new skills like first aid. Making the most of these opportunities and taking part in these activities can help you to decide what you want for your future. It can also improve your sense of belonging and wellbeing.

How gender can impact on your education

Last year you learned about sex and gender. Your sex and gender are an important part of who you are and can also affect some of your opportunities and experiences in life.

Read the following newspaper article, which explores how your education can be affected by your sex. As a class, discuss the questions that follow.

Students attending single-sex schools are more likely to go to university than those enrolled at co-ed schools, our figures show.

Although previous international studies have claimed that there is 'no scientific evidence' that single-sex schooling is better than co-ed, new findings, compiled by the *Sunday Independent*, suggest that more students from a single-sex education background are attending Irish universities.

Meanwhile, girls continue to outperform the boys at same-sex institutions as more females land university places.

Between 2009 and 2015, 81% of students at single-sex schools have furthered their education in the Republic and Northern Ireland. During the same period, 72% of students from mixed schools have furthered their education.

Around one-third of schools in Ireland are single-sex, a situation that is almost unique in Europe.

A gender breakdown of last year's Leaving Cert highlighted how girls continue to outperform boys – a trend that has been reflected across the globe over the past few decades.

Last year, female candidates produced more ABCs and fewer fails across almost all subjects, at both Higher and Ordinary Levels.

However, boys continue to have a distinct edge in maths and applied maths and also produced proportionately more top grades last year in Higher Level chemistry, Italian, engineering, construction studies and accounting.

Although there are mixed findings on the relative academic merits of single-sex versus mixed schools, there is more reliable evidence that co-education better prepares young people socially.

Source: Sunday Independent, 25 January 2016

1. Why do you think sex/gender can affect your performance in school?

2. Do you agree that a co-educational school better prepares young people socially?

Excellent

Work

■ Self-reflection ▮

In this lesson you will be focusing on the changes you have experienced during adolescence and how you have matured. You will have changed a lot in the last few years, but you may not realise it.

Complete the following activity to help you see how much you have matured in the last few years. You won't have to share your answers with the class.

Things I do	Most of the time	Sometimes	Almost never
I admit when I am wrong.			
I get along well with others.			
I help others to be their best.			
I take responsibility for my actions.			
I know my own strengths.			
I know my own weaknesses.			
I help around the house.			
I have my own values.			
I take care of my health.			
I form my own opinions.			
I ask for help when I have a problem.			
I don't blame other people when things are my fault.			
I am respectful in my relationships.			
I am a good friend.			
I accept compliments.			
I choose to be sexually healthy.			
I do my best.			
I can talk openly with friends or romantic partners.			
I enjoy regular exercise or activity.			
I can forgive myself.			
I am honest about how I feel.			
I take care of my own belongings.			

Mostly 'Most of the time'
Well done! You are a very mature individual and well on your way to becoming an adult.

Mostly 'Sometimes'
Good job! You are on your way to becoming a mature individual. Remember that you have more responsibilities now and don't be afraid to think for yourself.

Mostly 'Almost never'
In a few years' time you will officially be an adult, so start working on taking more responsibility for yourself.

Write down two areas from the list on the previous page that you could focus on improving this year.

_____

_____

Revisit the SPHE contract that you wrote in First Year and reviewed in Second Year. See if there is anything on it that you would like to change now.

My Life 1, Lesson 3

Write a positive message to Gemma, who feels that all her friends and peers are given responsibilities, but her parents still treat her like a child and won't let her stay at home by herself or cook dinner by herself.

_____

_____

_____

Rapid recap

3

Topics we discussed today:

1. _____

2. _____

3. _____

2

People or places I could find out more information on this lesson from:

1. _____

2. _____

1

Something in today's lesson that I would like to learn more about:

1. _____

Parent's/guardian's signature _____

(Your teacher will tell you if this should be signed each week.)

Describe yourself in three words.

_____

_____

_____

Complete your personal learning journal at home.

2. Planning for effective study

At the end of this lesson, you will:

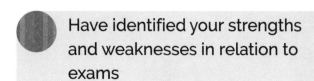 Have identified your strengths and weaknesses in relation to exams

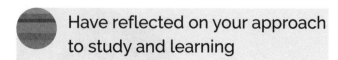 Have reflected on your approach to study and learning

 Have discussed exam stress and ways to deal with it

key words
abc **Exam stress**

Aware
Resilient

■ Study self-assessment ■

If you had to live on a desert island for a month and were only allowed to bring two personal items, what would they be? Tell your answer to the person beside you and explain why you chose these items.

Draw the following table in your copy. Complete the table for each exam subject that you are taking. One has already been done for you as an example.

Subject	Result	I am strongest in this section	I am weakest in this section
Home economics	C	Nutrition	Consumer studies

Answer the following questions.

1. What is your least favourite exam subject? _____
2. Do you usually run out of time during tests? Yes/No
3. What class do you get most distracted in? Why?_____
4. What subject do you usually get the best results in? _____
5. What subject do you spend most time on (homework/study)? _____
6. What is your favourite exam subject?_____
7. Does your teacher tell you that your answers lack detail? Yes/No
8. Do you sometimes misread or misunderstand the question? Yes/No
9. What subject do you spend the least amount of time on (homework/study)?_____
10. What subject do you get the worst results in? Why?_____
11. What class do you pay most attention in? Why?_____

Favourite subjects

Students often do well in the subject they like best. Students also tend to spend more time on this subject. Be aware of this when you are studying and doing homework, otherwise you will fall behind in the subjects that you don't like as much.

Reread the answers that you wrote to the questions on the previous page. Use these questions and answers to help you complete the next exercise.

Pretend that you are filling out your own report card. In the comment section, give yourself one piece of advice on how you could improve in each subject. For example: 'Must spend more time on long questions', 'More detailed answers needed' or 'Could show more interest in class'.

REPORT CARD

Subject	Comment

Exam stress

Some students find exams very stressful. Exam stress can be a result of worrying about how you will perform; pressure from yourself or others to do well; panic or fear that you have not done enough; or the hype about exams at home, in school or in the media. A certain amount of stress is good, as it helps you to work harder. Too much stress, however, can have a negative effect on your health. It can also prevent you from studying effectively and doing well in your exams.

Watch the video on FolensOnline where students discuss exam stress. In groups, discuss the following.

1. Do you agree or disagree that some students get stressed because they are worried about what friends and family will think about their exam results?

2. Do you agree or disagree with Ciara, who says that a certain amount of pressure is good?

1. Thinking back over what you have learned in First and Second Year, make a list of healthy ways to relieve stress during this year. Write your ideas here.

   _____
   _____
   _____
   _____
   _____

2. What can you do to help a friend or classmate who is really stressed about exams?

   _____
   _____
   _____
   _____
   _____

3. Discuss the best way to spend the evening before an important exam.

   _____
   _____
   _____
   _____
   _____

Write a positive message to Mike, who gets stressed about exams and finds it hard to sleep the night before a big exam.

_____

_____

_____

_____

Rapid recap

3

Topics we discussed today:

1. _____

2. _____

3. _____

2

People or places I could find out more information on this lesson from:

1. _____

2. _____

1

Something in today's lesson that I would like to learn more about:

1. _____

Parent's/guardian's signature _____

(Your teacher will tell you if this should be signed each week.)

Read the advice on preparing for exams on the SpunOut website. Write three pieces of that advice below.

_____

_____

_____

Complete your personal learning journal at home.

3. Setting goals for Third Year

At the end of this lesson, you will:

 Have set short-term and long-term goals for Third Year

 Have a greater appreciation of the factors that promote a good atmosphere for learning

key words
abc

Goal

Motivation

🧠 **Aware**
🏃 **Responsible**

What words do you think about or what feelings do you feel when you think about Junior Cycle exams and assessments? Write some of these on the whiteboard or do a brainstorm in your copy. Use symbols or pictures as well as words.

Looking back: Goals

Last year in Lesson 3, you learned about goals and set personal goals for Second Year. Can you remember what your goals were? Did you achieve your goals? Why or why not?

My Life 2, Lesson 3

You may remember that goals should be:

* Within your power to make happen through your own actions

* Important to you personally

* Something you have a reasonable chance of achieving

Goals can be short, medium or long term:

* A short-term goal could be getting your homework done by Friday.

* A medium-term goal could be running a 5k race in three months' time.

* A long-term goal could be practising the piano for 30 minutes every day so that you pass your exam next year.

A goal is something that you aim to achieve.

Answer the following questions in pairs.

1. Why is it important for young people to have goals when they are preparing for exams?

_____

_____

2. Give some examples of goals that a Third Year student might have.

_____

_____

3. Do you think parents and teachers put too much pressure on students in relation to school and exams?

_____

_____

1. Complete the table below in your copy, which is designed to help you achieve this important long-term goal.

My goal	To do well in my JCPA
To be achieved by	June
Steps I must take	
What might get in the way?	
Who can help me?	

2. Now set a short-term goal for this term and a medium-term goal for this year in a specific subject.

	Short-term goal	Medium-term goal
My goal		
To be achieved by	Midterm break	Christmas
Steps I need to take		
What might get in the way?		
Who can help me?		

Factors that promote learning

In order to achieve the goals that you have set for yourself in school, you need to understand the factors that promote learning.

Read the following list of factors that promote learning and discuss each one as a class.

Physical health

It is very important that you look after your physical health. Remember to eat well and take regular exercise. If you are unwell or always tired, it will be hard to learn and achieve your goals.

Mental health

Your mental health can become strained from stress and anxiety about study, projects and exams. Last year and in First Year you discussed ways you can deal with stress and you practised some stress-relieving techniques. Can you remember some of these?

As a class, discuss ways you can take care of your health this year. Write down some of the points in the table below.

How can I can take care of my physical health?	How can I take care of my mental health?

■ Staying motivated ■

It's hard to stay motivated. Sometimes you'll be tired of your teachers talking about assessment and exams. At times like that, try to remember why you are putting in all this hard work.

As a class, discuss some reasons that might motivate you to study and do well. Write some of them below.

_____

_____

_____

_____

_____

_____

■ Seeking help from others ■

You may find Third Year more stressful than previous years. It is overwhelming for a lot of students, so you are not alone. There are lots of people around you who can help.

Write down a list of people you could ask for help from during the year.

_____

_____

_____

_____

_____

_____

■ Your study environment ■

If you can't concentrate on your studies, it will lead to even more stress. It's hard to concentrate in loud environments. A good environment for learning should be quiet, comfortable and free of clutter. If your house is very noisy or if you don't have a room of your own to study in where you won't be interrupted, then try to find a better place to study.

As a class, discuss other places where you could study. Write them below.

_____

_____

_____

Write a positive message to Philip, who realises now at the beginning of Third Year that he wasted time during First and Second Year and never tried his best at schoolwork. Now he is afraid that it is too late to start trying.

_____

_____

_____

Rapid recap

3

Topics we discussed today:

1. _____

2. _____

3. _____

2

People or places I could find out more information on this lesson from:

1. _____

2. _____

1

Something in today's lesson that I would like to learn more about:

1. _____

Parent's/guardian's signature _____

(Your teacher will tell you if this should be signed each week.)

Answer the following questions.

1. This year, I will do the following to stay physically and mentally healthy:

_____

_____

2. When I get fed up studying or hearing about assessment or exams, I will remember that the hard work will be worth it because:

_____

_____

3. If I need help during the year, I will ask:

_____

_____

4. If I can't study at home, I will study:

_____

_____

Complete your personal learning journal at home.

4. Organising my time

At the end of this lesson, you will:

 Have analysed how you spend your time

 Have drawn up your own personal work contract

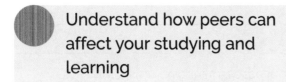 Understand how peers can affect your studying and learning

 Key words — abc — **Contract**

Aware

Responsible

Working in groups, you have 3 minutes to try to build the tallest structure in the class using a material of your teacher's choice. This could include paperclips, straws, paper, cards or books.

■ How do you spend your time? ■

1,2,3... Everybody obviously spends different amounts of time on various activities. However, these are the results from surveys on how young people in Ireland spend their time:

✳ A 2016 survey of 4,400 primary school children in Ireland found that 34% of them have more than two hours of screen time per day during weekdays. This figure rises to 54% having more than two hours of screen time per day at weekends.

✳ Four out of five children in the Republic of Ireland are not meeting the recommended guidelines for physical activity. (The recommended amount of physical activity for school-aged children is at least 60 minutes per day.)

✳ Only 12% of post-primary school children are meeting the current recommendation of 60 minutes of moderate to vigorous physical activity daily.

✳ The average amount of time that pre-school children spend watching TV every day is 2.2 hours.

✳ In 1981, 50% of school-going children walked to school. By 2014, that figure had been cut in half, to 25%.

✳ Irish teens spend more time doing homework than most of their counterparts in developed countries. Fifteen-year-olds here reported doing more than seven hours a week on average. In most OECD countries, the average is five hours.

✳ The average person in Ireland sleeps for 7 hours and 16 minutes each night. (The research carried out by alarm clock app Sleep Cycle found that Japanese people sleep less than any other nation on Earth, with only 5 hours and 52 minutes of sleep each night.)

In pairs, discuss the following.

1. What activities do you think you spend too much time on?

2. Is there any activity that you gave up that you used to enjoy?

3. How much sleep do you usually get?

4. Do you ever try to put off doing study or homework by doing something else?

5. Some internet service providers have a feature that allows parents to block access to gaming and social networking sites during their teenager's study time. Do you think this is a good idea?

Make the most of your study time

Study for short periods

If you try to do too much studying at one time, you will tire yourself out and your studying won't be very effective. Take a 10-minute break every 45 minutes – set an alarm as a reminder.

Plan specific times for studying

Schedule specific times throughout the week for your study time. Stick to these times even if you don't feel like studying then. Studying at the same time each day establishes a routine that becomes a regular part of your life, just like sleeping and eating.

Set specific goals for each study session

Goals will help you to stay focused and monitor your progress. You must be very clear about what you want to accomplish during your study session, for example knowing the functions of all the nutrients or being able to answer all the question 1s. Remember to set realistic goals for yourself.

Study the most difficult thing first

Your most difficult assignment will require the most effort. Start with your most difficult subject or question, since this is when you have the most mental energy.

Assessment idea

1,2,3... Conduct a survey or report on study and homework in your school or year. Topics could include the amount of time Sixth or Third Years spend on homework or study, the subject students find most difficult to study, teachers' opinions on the importance of homework or study, etc.

Personal work contract

In the previous lesson, you set yourself goals for Third Year. Drawing up and signing a contract encourages you to work towards achieving those goals. Complete this personal work contract. After you've signed it, ask your parent/guardian and your class tutor to sign it. Try to be realistic. Only set goals that you think are achievable.

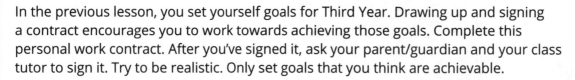

Personal work contract

This year I promise to...

Spend _____ hours on homework or study every night except for _____

_____

Spend less time _____

_____

Spend more time _____

_____

I will take care of my health by _____

_____

I will cut down on _____

_____

I promise to talk to _____ if I am finding things hard.

Signed: _____ Date: _____

Parent/guardian signature: _____

Class tutor signature: _____

abc Contract
A document that records an agreement.

Making the most of class time

Your peers can have a positive or negative effect on your attitude and approach to studying and learning. Sometimes peer pressure is easy to see; other times it is not. Try not to let your peers have a negative effect on how you study or learn. Also, don't put pressure on your peers that stops them from learning.

How do your peers have a negative effect on your studying and learning? As a class, agree on three ways you can create a positive learning environment in your class/year.

_____

_____

_____

Write a positive message to Karla, who wants to study but finds it hard to concentrate and always ends up looking at stuff on the internet instead.

_____

_____

_____

Rapid recap

3

Topics we discussed today:

1. _____

2. _____

3. _____

2

People or places I could find out more information on this lesson from:

1. _____

2. _____

1

Something in today's lesson that I would like to learn more about:

1. _____

Parent's/guardian's signature _____

(Your teacher will tell you if this should be signed each week.)

Discuss your goals for this year with your parent/guardian. Ask them to read and sign your personal work contract on page 24. Discuss ways your parent/guardian can help you to study. You may also like to make a study timetable for this term.

WHAT ARE YOUR GOALS

Complete your personal learning journal at home.

5. Deciding on subjects and careers

At the end of this lesson, you will:

 Apply decision-making skills to choices about your subjects and future career

 Consider the consequences of choosing a particular subject

Key words
abc

Career

Consequence

Interpersonal skills

CAREER

CAREER

CAREER

Aware

Responsible

You have discovered a magic genie who can make three wishes come true. Working in groups, your group must agree on the three wishes. You have 5 minutes before the magic genie disappears. If everyone in the group does not agree on the wishes, they will not come true. What will you wish for? Remember that each wish will have a consequence.

■ Career choice ■

In the next year or so, you will have to choose the subjects that you want to do for your Leaving Certificate. Choosing subjects is an important decision because it sets you on a new path to college and to your career.

Read the list of jobs below as a class and see if you can add more to the list. Cross out any careers you are definitely not interested in, then circle the jobs that you would like to find out more about.

Doctor **Farmer** *Tour guide*

Sales representative **Architect** *Journalist* Nail technician

Musician **Plumber** CHEF **Mechanic**

Artist **Greens keeper** Forester NURSE

Sports professional **Accountant**

Business manager

Jeweller MIDWIFE Hairdresser Driver

Business owner Pilot **Garda** Surveyor

Personal trainer

Actor Librarian

Veterinarian

Teacher Model **Bar worker**

Counsellor *Economist* HOTEL MANAGER

Lawyer CHILDCARE WORKER Electrician Banker

Fire-fighter *Computer programmer*

Historian Fashion designer **Builder**

Career adviser

Beautician *Engineer*

Travel agent

Nanny **Carpenter** Physiotherapist

Electronics technician Dentist

Shopkeeper **Occupational therapist**

Social worker MAKE-UP ARTIST Scientist

Singer Pharmacist/chemist School principal

1. In groups, talk about people you know who have a really great job. Tell the others about it and how they got that job if you know.

2. Think about what your dream job would be, then tell the others in the group about it.

■ Work experience ■

Work experience is a great way to improve your coping skills, as you will have to make important decisions by yourself. It can also be a fantastic way to improve your social and interpersonal skills.

If you are doing Transition Year (TY) next year or Leaving Certificate Vocational Programme (LCVP) in Fifth Year, you will be doing work experience at some stage. If you are not doing TY or LCVP, then perhaps you will be getting a summer job at some stage.

It's a good idea to try to get work experience or have a summer job in an area that you are interested in as a career to see if you really like it. It's also a great way of making contacts with companies you may want to work for when you qualify.

abc **Interpersonal skills** are the skills used to communicate and interact with other people, both individually and in groups.

Choose three of the careers that you have not crossed off the list on page 29. Think of three places where you could look for work experience or a summer job that would relate to these careers. Write them in the table below.

Career	Where can I do work experience?

Choosing subjects for Transition Year or Leaving Certificate

There are consequences involved in taking or not taking a particular subject or level. For example, there are more than 1,000 courses that you *cannot* do if you don't have at least an O1 in maths. You can check the subjects required for entry into all courses online.

Find all of the subjects that you can choose from next year. Fill out the table below to help you decide which subjects you might choose. Some subjects will be compulsory, so you don't need to include these in the table.

Subject	Do I like it? (Y/N)	Am I good at it? (Y/N)	Will I need it for the college courses and careers I'm thinking about? (Y/N)

Does anyone have an older brother or sister who is doing or has done the Leaving Certificate? What subjects did they choose? Make a list of people who can help you decide which subjects to do.

_____

_____

_____

If you are unsure about a subject, these questions will help you to make a clear decision.

* **Who is influencing you?** Are you being influenced by teachers, parents or friends? Do they have your best interests at heart?

* **Are you in a good state of mind?** If you leave the decision until the last minute, you won't be thinking clearly.

* **What are your reasons?** Do you want to do a subject because it is easy, because you like it or because your friends are doing it? Will you do a lower level than you are able to do because you are lazy or will you always try to do your best?

* **What are the consequences of the decision?** How will doing or not doing a certain subject affect your choice of college course and your workload?

abc ⚷

Consequence
Something that happens as a result of your decisions or actions.

Find out more about choosing subjects that suit your skills on FolensOnline.

Write a positive message to Anne. Nobody in her family has ever studied at third level. She really wants to, but she is afraid to tell them in case they laugh at her.

_____

_____

_____

_____

_____

Rapid recap

3

Topics we discussed today:

1. _____

2. _____

3. _____

2

People or places I could find out more information on this lesson from:

1. _____

2. _____

1

Something in today's lesson that I would like to learn more about:

1. _____

Parent's/guardian's signature _____

(Your teacher will tell you if this should be signed each week.)

Go to the Careers Portal website to help you find the following information. Choose one career that you are interested in and answer the following questions.

1. What course will I have to apply for? (There may be many, so pick one.)

   _____

2. Where is this course taught?

   _____

3. What subjects do I need for this course?

   _____

4. How many years is the course?

   _____

5. How many points does it look like I will need for this course?

   _____

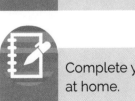

Complete your personal learning journal at home.

█ Strand review

In this strand, you learned about:

- Being you
- Planning for effective study
- Setting goals for Third Year
- Organising your time
- Deciding on subjects and careers

Look back over the lessons that you completed. In the table below, tick the skills that you think you learned or used.

Managing myself

- I know myself better. ◯
- I made decisions. ◯
- I set goals. ◯
- I achieved goals. ◯
- I thought about what I learned. ◯
- I used technology to learn. ◯

Staying well

- I am healthy and active. ◯
- I am social. ◯
- I feel safe. ◯
- I am spiritual. ◯
- I feel confident. ◯
- I feel positive about what I learned. ◯

Communicating

- I used language. ◯
- I used numbers. ◯
- I listened to my classmates. ◯
- I expressed myself. ◯
- I performed/ presented. ◯
- I had a discussion/ debate. ◯
- I used technology to communicate. ◯

Being literate

- I understand some new words. ◯
- I enjoyed words and language. ◯
- I wrote for different reasons. ◯
- I expressed my ideas clearly. ◯
- I developed my spoken language. ◯
- I read and wrote in different ways. ◯

Being creative

- I used my imagination. ◯
- I thought about things from a different point of view. ◯
- I put ideas into action. ◯
- I learned in a creative way. ◯
- I was creative with digital technology. ◯

Working with others

- I developed relationships. ◯
- I dealt with conflict. ◯
- I co-operated. ◯
- I respected difference. ◯
- I helped make the world a better place. ◯
- I learned with others. ◯
- I worked with others using digital technology. ◯

Managing information and thinking

- I was curious. ◯
- I gathered and analysed information. ◯
- I thought creatively. ◯
- I thought about what I learned. ◯
- I used digital technology to access, manage and share information. ◯

Being numerate

- I expressed ideas mathematically. ◯
- I estimated, predicted and calculated. ◯
- I was interested in problem-solving. ◯
- I saw patterns and trends. ◯
- I gathered and presented data. ◯
- I used digital technology to review and understand numbers. ◯

Now write two skills from the list that you think you should focus on more in the future.

_____

_____

Minding myself and others

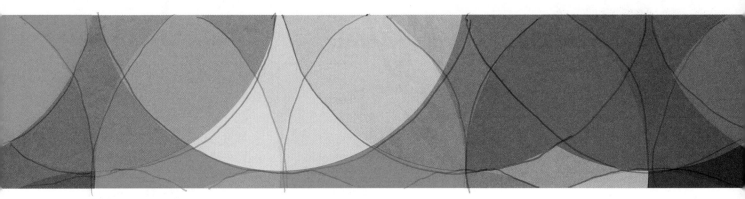

This strand provides opportunities for you to reflect on how you can best take care of yourself and others.

Strand learning outcomes

- Evaluate how diet, physical activity, sleep/rest and hygiene contribute to self-confidence, self-esteem and wellbeing

- Critique the impact of the media, advertising and other influences on your decisions about health and wellbeing

- Describe what promotes a sense of belonging in school, at home and in the wider community and your own role in creating an inclusive environment

- Distinguish between appropriate care giving and receiving

- Demonstrate the personal and social skills to address pressure to smoke, to drink alcohol and/or to use other substances

- Reflect on the personal, social and legal consequences of your own or others' drug use

- Critique information and supports available for young people in relation to substance use

- Use good communication skills to respond to criticism and conflict

- Review the school's anti-bullying policy and internet safety guidelines explaining the implications for students' behaviour and personal safety

6. Eating well

At the end of this lesson, you will:

 Understand how to examine a nutritional label

 Appreciate the importance of choosing a healthy breakfast

 Know how to plan a healthy lunch

Key words

Nutritional label

Aware
Responsible

⬚ A healthy breakfast ⊏⊐

Play the following memory game: 'My granny went shopping and bought me a …'. Each person in turn should repeat what the previous students have said, then add an item to the list. Every item should be a food item. Who can remember the most?

Breakfast is an important meal. If you haven't eaten for a long time you can be more tired and weak, which can make it difficult to concentrate and learn in school. There are many unhealthy breakfast cereals on the market aimed at children and teenagers that are very high in sugar and low in fibre. You may remember from last year that fibre makes you feel fuller for longer, helps food move through the intestines and prevents bowel diseases, which are very common in Ireland. Sugar causes tooth decay and weight gain. Therefore, a healthy breakfast should be high in fibre and low in sugar.

1. In pairs, discuss what you normally eat for breakfast.

   _____

2. Do you have a different breakfast at weekends or during holidays?

   _____

3. What is your favourite breakfast?

   _____

4. How do you feel if you haven't eaten for a long time?

   _____

Nutritional labels

As a class, go online to look up some nutritional labels from popular breakfast cereals. First look at the colours, words and characters on the box – who is this breakfast cereal aimed at? Next, find out the fibre and sugar content. On the packet it may show you the fibre and sugar content per 30 gram serving. Most people would eat about 60 grams of a breakfast cereal as a portion.

1,2,3... Look at the example below. You will see that under carbohydrates, of which sugars, it says 17 grams for a 30 gram portion. So if you ate a 60 gram portion it would have 34 grams of sugar, which is equivalent to 7 teaspoons of sugar! There are 0.6 grams of fibre in a 30 gram serving, so a 60 gram serving would have 1.2 grams of fibre.

> **A nutritional label**
> is a label found on most packaged foods. It shows the amount of each nutrient in a set amount of the food, e.g. how much protein is in 100 grams of that food.

Home Economics

Nutrition Information		
○ Typical value per 100 g	○ Per 30 g serving with 125 ml of semi-skimmed milk	
ENERGY	1639 kJ / 387 kcal	743 kJ / 175 kcal
PROTEIN	5 g	6 g
CARBOHYDRATE	85 g	32 g
of which sugars	35 g	17 g
starch	50 g	15 g
FAT	2.5 g	3 g
of which saturates	1 g	11.5 g
FIBRE	2 g	0.6 g
SODIUM	0.3 g	0.15 g
SALT	0.75 g	0.35 g
VITAMINS:	(% RDA)	(% RDA)
VITAMIN D	4.2 µg (83)	1.3 µg (25)
THIAMIN (B_1)	0.9 mg (83)	0.3 mg (30)
RIBOFLAVIN (B_2)	1.2 mg (83)	0.7 mg (47)
NIACIN	13.3 mg (83)	4.2 mg (26)
VITAMIN B_6	1.2 mg (83)	0.4 mg (31)
FOLIC ACID	166 µg (83)	58 µg (29)
VITAMIN B_{12}	2.1 µg (83)	1.2 µg (46)

Use the table below to help you figure out which breakfast cereals or cereal bars that you looked up online are healthier choices. Remember, you want one that is low in sugar and high in fibre. Write the healthier choices below.

Per 100g	Low	Medium	High
Sugar	5 grams or less	5.1–15 grams	More than 15 grams
Fibre	1–2 grams	2.1–6 grams	More than 6 grams

_____

_____

Suggested healthy breakfasts

Porridge with milk and mixed berries
(try adding one of the following: cinnamon,
yogurt, 1 teaspoon of honey or sugar, raisins,
mashed banana, seeds or chopped nuts)

***

Weetabix with milk and fruit

***

Poached eggs on brown toast

***

Scrambled eggs with granary toast and grilled rasher,
mushrooms and tomato

***

Overnight oats (oats soaked in yogurt and fruit
overnight)

***

Wholegrain toast with banana

A healthy lunch

At this age, you are well able to make your own lunch. It is up to you to try to make it as healthy and filling as possible. If you want some healthier choices for your lunch, you should talk to your parents/guardians about this before they do their shopping.

In First Year you learned about the food pyramid (see *My Life 1*, page 46). The food pyramid is a useful guide to help you pack a healthy lunch.

My Life 1, Lesson 8

You should try to include four of the five food groups below in your lunchbox every day.

	Example	More ideas
1 fruit (not a juice)	An apple	An orange
1 vegetable	Carrot sticks	
1 milk/cheese or yogurt	Cheese sandwich on brown bread	Cold pasta salad with chicken and sweetcorn
1 wholegrain bread, rice, pasta or potato		
1 meat, poultry, fish, eggs, beans or nuts		

In groups, design four more healthy lunches suitable for school. Remember, you should include four out of the five foods from the above table. Write them in your copy.

Go to the Irish Heart Foundation website and read about the 'Stop targeting kids' campaign. Watch the videos, then as a class discuss how advertising on TV, bus shelters, social media and magazines affects your food choices.

Assessment idea

Prepare a presentation or information booklet for First Years on healthy lunches. Use Lesson 8 from *My Life 1* to help explain the food pyramid and portion sizes. Give examples of healthy lunches and advice on choosing healthy options from your school cafeteria or shop. The Bord Bia, Food Dudes and Safefood websites might help too.

🔗 *My Life 1*, Lesson 8

Write a positive message to Lara, who wants to eat a healthy lunch every day, but when it comes to preparing it she usually just grabs something easy that morning or forgets and has to ask her mam for money to buy a sausage roll and chips in the school canteen.

_____

_____

_____

Rapid recap

3

Topics we discussed today:

1. _____

2. _____

3. _____

2

People or places I could find out more information on this lesson from:

1. _____

2. _____

1

Something in today's lesson that I would like to learn more about:

1. _____

Parent's/guardian's signature _____

(Your teacher will tell you if this should be signed each week.)

Plan two healthy changes that you will make to your lunch or breakfast this week. Report back to the class next week on how it went.

_____

_____

Complete your personal learning journal at home.

7. Staying well

At the end of this lesson, you will:

 Be aware of the impact of mental and physical exercise on health

 Appreciate the importance of showing kindness to others and to yourself

Key words
abc

Exercise

♥ **Active**

💡 **Aware**

🤲 **Connected**

Take a brisk 5-minute walk around your school. How did you feel afterwards?

Exercise your brain

In the last lesson, you learned about choosing a healthy lunch and breakfast to help you stay well. Over the last two years in SPHE you have also learned a lot about maintaining a healthy mind, such as recognising and dealing with stress, practising positive thinking and developing positive self-esteem. In this lesson we will examine some of the lifestyle choices that you will face that will also affect your overall health and wellbeing.

Playing games or doing activities that exercise your brain has many benefits. You might often feel that you have no time for these types of games or puzzles as you have enough schoolwork to do. However, doing some type of mental exercise in the form of brain teasers or word and number games can be an excellent way to improve your study skills and learning power by:

✴ Boosting overall brain activity

✴ Increasing your memory power

✴ Improving memory and brain processing speed

✴ Reducing boredom

✴ Improving concentration

Studies have found that playing computer games doesn't have the same effect. People who play these games might get better at the tasks they practise while playing, but the games don't seem to improve users' overall brain skills, such as concentration, memory, use of language and ability to navigate.

In pairs, make a list of some brain games or puzzles that you could do at home.

_____

_____

_____

_____

_____

_____

_____

Exercise your body

You may remember from Lesson 9 in *My Life 1* that teenagers should be active for at least 60 minutes every day. If you play sports, that is a fantastic way to stay fit. Not everybody enjoys sports, however, so below is a list of other ways to stay active.

 PE *My Life 1*, Lesson 9

 In groups, discuss each activity on the list. Go online to find out if there are classes offered in any of these activities in your area. Discuss whether the activities would be expensive or inexpensive to do. Discuss whether these activities would be suitable for people with various disabilities.

- Aqua aerobics or aquatics
- Archery
- Dancing
- Fencing
- Frisbee
- Hill walking
- Horse riding
- Hula hooping
- Martial arts
- Orienteering
- Pilates
- Rock climbing
- Sailing
- Trampolining
- Walking
- Yoga

Be kind

Religion

Possibly one of the most important things in life is being kind to yourself and others. Sometimes we are so busy or caught up in our own thoughts or worries that we forget about being kind. Each act of kindness, no matter how small, actually changes the way we see ourselves, the way we see others and the way others see us. Kindness doesn't have to cost money. It can be a simple smile, sharing something, making someone feel welcome or making someone's day a little bit easier.

When our kind actions affect the lives of others, we feel better about ourselves – more confident, useful and positive. At the same time, we may also feel less stressed about our own problems because we are doing our part to make a difference. In our normal lives, we may find ourselves feeling more grateful for what we have and more positive about the future.

By always trying to be kind, we become a different person – and others notice that. We become more likable, more trusted and more worthy of kindness ourselves, thus completing the circle of kindness.

Think about and discuss ways that you can be kind to the following people:

- A parent/guardian
- A sibling or cousin
- A cleaner in your school
- A friend who is upset about something
- An elderly neighbour
- A stranger
- A student in your class who is always on their own
- A cashier in a shop
- Yourself

Write a positive message to Isaac, who thinks that his older brother hates him as he has never said or done a kind thing to him in his life.

_____

_____

_____

Rapid recap

3

Topics we discussed today:

1. _____

2. _____

3. _____

2

People or places I could find out more information on this lesson from:

1. _____

2. _____

1

Something in today's lesson that I would like to learn more about:

1. _____

Parent's/guardian's signature _____

(Your teacher will tell you if this should be signed each week.)

 In your personal learning journal, write about a time when you were kind to someone or someone was kind to you.

 Complete your personal learning journal at home.

8. Dealing with conflict and criticism

At the end of this lesson, you will:

 Have further developed your communication skills by learning how to use constructive criticism

 Have enhanced your skills for dealing with conflict

Conflict

Constructive criticism

Criticism

Aware
Connected
Resilient

_____

_____

_____

_____

Constructive criticism

People use constructive criticism to help someone better themselves. It is generally intended to be helpful to the person being criticised. For example, a teacher might criticise your handwriting because they want you to get better exam results.

Constructive criticism

abc

Advice or feedback that is useful and intended to help or improve something.

If someone offers you constructive criticism, try to use it to your advantage. Focus on developing the good points and work on improving the bad points. Don't be offended – the person is probably trying to be helpful. Criticism can be hard to hear, especially when you worked hard on something, but try to be gracious and thank the person for their advice.

Negative criticism

Negative criticism is often intended to hurt the other person's feelings and is sometimes harsh and insulting. An example of negative criticism is a 'friend' telling you that your new haircut is awful. If someone criticises you harshly rather than in a nice or constructive way, they are probably trying to make you feel bad about yourself, so try your best to ignore it.

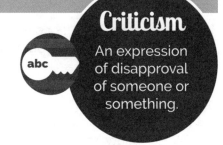

Criticism

An expression of disapproval of someone or something.

Discuss the worst reactions from contestants to criticism on TV talent shows. Were the judges being constructive or negative and hurtful?

Using constructive criticism

If used properly, constructive criticism can really help people. A true friend can use it to save a friend from embarrassment. Follow the guidelines below to use constructive criticism properly.

* **Choose the right time.** For example, don't tell someone they can't act just before they are due to perform on stage.

* **Be sensitive about how the criticism might make them feel.** Don't say it in front of other people.

* **Be specific and offer advice.** For example, 'I liked the story you wrote. It was funny, but I didn't really understand the ending. Maybe you could explain it a bit better?'

* **Share something about yourself.** For example, say something like, 'I think that an A-line dress would suit you better. I used to think I looked great in body con dresses until I saw a photo of myself and I looked awful.' This way, the person won't feel as bad and will realise that you really are only trying to help.

In pairs, discuss how you could use constructive criticism in the following situations. Write what you would say and think about how your friend might feel if you said it.

Situation 1

Your friend Mick plays the guitar well but sings very badly. You have heard other people in the class making fun of his singing and you have to admit that he really is very bad. His dad keeps telling him that he is an excellent singer and musician. He is even talking about entering *The X Factor* – he wants to play guitar and sing a ballad. He asks you to help him choose a song to sing. You really don't want him to embarrass himself in front of all those people. What should you say?

_____

_____

_____

Situation 2

Your friend Anna has bought a new dress for your friend's sixteenth birthday party. It is very tight and is short red satin. She thinks it looks really classy and expensive and that it makes her legs look great. You think that it looks cheap and that it makes her look much bigger than she really is. The party is tomorrow night and you don't want to hurt her feelings, but you don't want her to look awful. What should you say?

_____

_____

_____

▨ Dealing with conflict ▨

Last year, you learned about dealing with conflict in your family. We are now going to revisit that topic and learn more about dealing with conflict.

↻ *My Life 2*, Lesson 9

Conflict is not pleasant, but it is a part of our lives. Sometimes you are constantly in conflict with people you might not like or have much in common with. Other times you might find yourself at odds with someone you care about a lot, like a friend or family member. No matter what the situation is, there are strategies you can use to help resolve conflict situations.

▨ Tips for resolving conflict ▨

Can you remember some of the tips for resolving conflict in your family from last year? Read the tips again in *My Life 2*, Lesson 9, if necessary before doing the next activity, which examines conflict in a romantic relationship. The situation is different, but the guidelines for dealing with conflict are the same.

↻ *My Life 2*, Lesson 9

Conflict

abc A disagreement or difference between people.

Last year you learned about Áine and Mark's relationship and the conflict they experienced. Watch the video again on FolensOnline and discuss the following in your groups.

1. What was the cause of conflict in the relationship?

2. Do you think Áine dealt with her feelings in an appropriate way?

Now watch the next part of Áine and Mark's story and write down the answers to the following questions.

3. How did Áine and Mark solve the conflict in their relationship?

   _____

   _____

4. Based on what you have seen in Áine and Mark's story, write three pieces of advice for teenagers on how to resolve conflict in relationships.

   _____

   _____

   _____

Write a positive message to Paul, who is annoyed with his friend for telling others an embarrassing story about him. Paul wants his friend to know he is upset, but he hates any type of confrontation.

_____

_____

_____

Rapid recap

3

Topics we discussed today:

1. _____

2. _____

3. _____

2

People or places I could find out more information on this lesson from:

1. _____

2. _____

1

Something in today's lesson that I would like to learn more about:

1. _____

Parent's/guardian's signature _____

(Your teacher will tell you if this should be signed each week.)

Complete the following in your personal learning journal.

1. Write about one piece of constructive criticism you have received. How did it make you feel? Did it help you to improve anything about yourself?

2. Write about a time when someone gave you negative criticism. How did it make you feel? Do you think they were trying to be mean? Why?

Complete your personal learning journal at home.

9. Roles and responsibilities at home

At the end of this lesson, you will:

 Have analysed your responsibilities at home

 Understand and appreciate the role of young carers

 Know how to support young carers

 Know where you can get help if you are a young carer

Key words

Responsibility

Role

Aware

Connected

Resilient

Roles and responsibilities at home

Last year you learned about roles and responsibilities that you may have at home. Remember, a **role** means the position occupied in the family, for example brother or mother. **Responsibilities** are the duties attached to a role, for example a parent should care for the children.

 My Life 2, Lesson 9

Sometimes teenagers have responsibilities that they don't like, such as cleaning their bedrooms. Other times parents don't give them any responsibilities because it is sometimes easier and less hassle for parents to do the job themselves or because they may not think you are able to do it.

CSPE

In the table below, tick the responsibilities that you have. Add some more to the list.

Responsibility	Is this one of my responsibilities?
Cleaning my room	
Making my school lunch	
Clearing up after dinner	
Making dinner for the family	
Deciding when I should go to bed	
Helping to care for another family member	
Deciding how long I should spend on study or homework	
Making my breakfast	
Paying for my own luxury items, e.g. phone credit, computer games, make-up	
Deciding what time I should come home at	

As a class, discuss whether you think you have the correct amount of responsibility in your home. Would you like to be responsible for things but your parents won't let you?

Ryan's story

Read the following story about Ryan, who has the role of carer in his home.

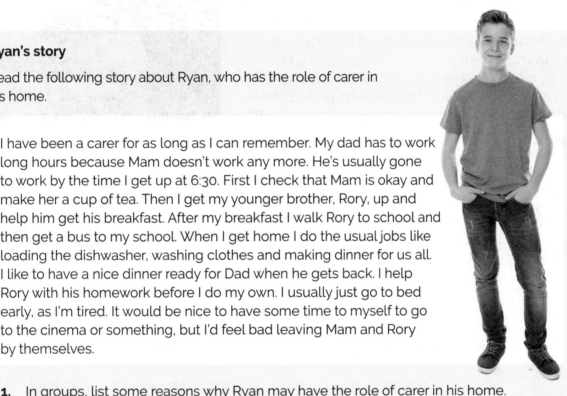

I have been a carer for as long as I can remember. My dad has to work long hours because Mam doesn't work any more. He's usually gone to work by the time I get up at 6:30. First I check that Mam is okay and make her a cup of tea. Then I get my younger brother, Rory, up and help him get his breakfast. After my breakfast I walk Rory to school and then get a bus to my school. When I get home I do the usual jobs like loading the dishwasher, washing clothes and making dinner for us all. I like to have a nice dinner ready for Dad when he gets back. I help Rory with his homework before I do my own. I usually just go to bed early, as I'm tired. It would be nice to have some time to myself to go to the cinema or something, but I'd feel bad leaving Mam and Rory by themselves.

1. In groups, list some reasons why Ryan may have the role of carer in his home.

_____

_____

_____

2. What extra responsibilities does he have?

_____

_____

_____

3. How do you think his role and responsibilities affect him?

_____

_____

_____

Young carers

Young carers are children or young people under the age of 18 who care or help to care for somebody in their family with a disability, illness or mental health illness or who has an alcohol or drug problem. If you are a young carer you may help care for a parent, sibling, grandparent or other relative.

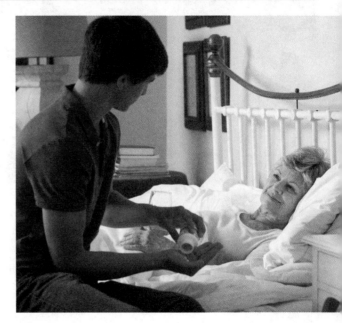

Young carers have additional responsibilities at home, such as cleaning, cooking, helping with medicines, keeping the person safe, bathing or dressing them or just making sure they are okay. Most young carers enjoy caring and are proud of what they do. Being a carer often makes them more mature and responsible than their peers. Sometimes, though, being a young carer can be too much to handle. It can affect how they feel or how much time they get to spend with friends or doing their schoolwork. Young carers often need some help.

Go to the Young Carers website and read and watch the stories about young carers. You will also find many more videos online if you search for 'a day in the life of a young carer'.

1. After reading or watching the stories, list some extra responsibilities that these young carers have in their lives.

   _____

   _____

2. List some problems or difficulties that they experience.

   _____

   _____

Research suggests that about 12% of young people are young carers. What is 12% of your school population? If you had a friend who was a young carer, how might you support them?

Finding help

* If you are a young carer and are finding things hard, you can talk to your class tutor or school counsellor.

* The Young Carers office runs a support line for young carers and opportunities to access day events, training, leadership programmes, competitions, counselling and other supports.

* If you are a carer due to a problem drinker at home, you can contact Alateen. This is a service for young people aged 12 to 17 who are affected by a problem drinker.

Young carers do an amazing job at home and in our communities, but this often goes unrecognised. Discuss ways that young carers in your school could be supported and recognised.

Write a positive message to Miro, who is a young carer and is finding Third Year difficult as he has little time to study. He is afraid to say anything to his teachers in case they think he isn't a good son.

_____

_____

_____

Rapid recap

3

Topics we discussed today:

1. _____

2. _____

3. _____

2

People or places I could find out more information on this lesson from:

1. _____

2. _____

1

Something in today's lesson that I would like to learn more about:

1. _____

Parent's/guardian's signature _____

(Your teacher will tell you if this should be signed each week.)

Go to the Young Carers website and find out three facts or statistics about young carers in Ireland.

_____

_____

_____

Complete your personal learning journal at home.

10. Taking care online

At the end of this lesson, you will:

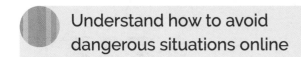 Understand how to avoid dangerous situations online

 Have reviewed cyberbullying

Have identified other online situations that might be unsafe

Appreciate the importance of respectful cyber communication with teachers

 Key words abc

Cyberbullying
Phishing
Identity theft

Aware
Responsible

Design your own formula for making fun usernames for online accounts. For example, a username that combines your favourite colour, your middle name and your favourite food could be pinkrosiechips!

Looking back: Cyberbullying

Last year you learned about cyberbullying.

My Life 2, Lesson 15

1. In groups, explain cyberbullying and its effects. Give three examples in your explanation.

_____

_____

_____

2. Write down three things you should do if you experience online bullying.

_____

_____

_____

Phishing and spam emails

Phishing is an illegal activity that involves someone trying to get information such as usernames, passwords or credit card details (and sometimes, indirectly, money) online or by phone by pretending to be a trustworthy person or company. Phishing emails may contain links to websites that are infected with viruses. Go to the Webwise website to find out more about communicating safely online.

Have you heard stories about people who were victims of a phishing scam? Or has anyone in the class ever received calls or texts from dodgy sources looking for personal information? Share your stories with each other. Discuss what you can do to prevent phishing or scam emails.

Social media and social networking sites

Sites and apps like Instagram, Facebook and Snapchat let people connect with others to share information like photos, videos and personal messages. While this makes communication with friends easier, you need to be aware that dangerous people such as hackers, virus writers, identity thieves and other criminals can follow what you write. Follow the tips below to help protect yourself when you use social networks.

Social media safety

* **Don't trust that a message is really from who it says it's from.** Hackers can break into accounts and send messages that look like they're from your friends.

* **Be careful what you post about yourself.** A common way that hackers break into accounts is by clicking the 'Forgot your password?' link on the account login page. To break into your account, they search for the answers to your security questions, such as your birthday or your mother's maiden name.

* **Be selective about who you accept as a friend on a social network.** Identity thieves might create fake profiles in order to get information from you.

* **Assume that everything you put on a social networking site is permanent.** Even if you can delete your account, anyone on the internet can easily print photos or text or save images and videos to a computer.

Identity theft is a crime where someone steals your personal information and uses it to their advantage, for example to buy things online or to get a loan.

Has anyone ever had their social networking site hacked? Has anyone you know ever been a victim of identity theft?

Respectful cyber communication with your teachers

You may need to email assessments to teachers or communicate with them regarding other schoolwork or extracurricular activities. Read your school's internet safety guidelines or internet usage policy. Are there guidelines on respectful online communication with teachers?

As a class, discuss whether or not the following are appropriate and respectful ways to communicate with your teacher.

- Ask them to be a friend on a social networking site
- Text them to say you are sick and can't play a match
- Send them private messages on their social networking pages
- Email them to find out what you missed in school that day
- Email them a school project
- Post a photo of a teacher on your social media page

1. In pairs, read the following email sent by a student to a teacher. Circle the parts that you think may be disrespectful or inappropriate.

To: SPHEteacher@saintmaryschool.com

From: cheekybunny@hotmail.com

2:37 a.m.

Subject: Hi ☺

Hiya Ms M, here's d thing we were supposed to hand in yesterday, sorry it's late, just remembered when i got home from disco.

C ya 2 moro xx

2. Rewrite the email appropriately in your copy.

Assessment idea

Write a list of guidelines for incoming First Years on one of the following:

- Respectful cyber communication with teachers
- Shopping safely online
- Putting a stop to cyberbullying

Write a positive message to Tess, who accidentally used her parents' credit card on a website that she now realises was not genuine. She doesn't want to tell her parents in case they won't let her use the internet any more.

_____

_____

_____

Rapid recap

3

Topics we discussed today:

1. _____

2. _____

3. _____

2

People or places I could find out more information on this lesson from:

1. _____

2. _____

1

Something in today's lesson that I would like to learn more about:

1. _____

Parent's/guardian's signature _____

(Your teacher will tell you if this should be signed each week.)

If you use a social networking site, check it tonight to see if you have given away any important personal information that could be used by an identity thief. Examples include:

- Your full name
- Your address
- Your phone number
- Your date of birth
- The names of your parents/guardians

Complete your personal learning journal at home.

11. Alcohol

At the end of this lesson, you will:

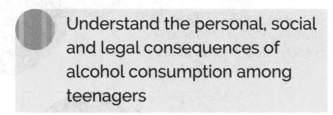
Understand the personal, social and legal consequences of alcohol consumption among teenagers

Know where to get help with alcohol-related issues

Key words
abc

Blood alcohol concentration

Physical effect

Psychological effect

Aware
Responsible

■ What happens when you drink alcohol? ■

The amount of alcohol in your body is measured by blood alcohol concentration (BAC). BAC is determined by the amount of alcohol you drink, how fast you drink, your weight, gender, drinking habits and whether you have eaten any food. The same amount of alcohol consumed will result in different blood alcohol levels for different people.

The table on the next page shows how alcohol affects people physically and psychologically according to their BAC. Discuss the stages of drunkenness in the table and the dangers associated with each effect that alcohol has on the body.

Home Economics

Psychological effect
abc
A change in the mind.

Physical effect
abc
A change in the body.

Blood alcohol concentration (BAC) % by volume	Physical effects	Psychological effects
0.1–0.5% (Note: The legal BAC limit for driving in Ireland is 0.5.)	• Quicker heart and breathing rate • Slower reactions • Less able to carry out simple tasks	• Decrease in judgement • Loss of inhibitions • Mild sense of happiness, relaxation and pleasure
0.6–1%	• Tiredness • Poor co-ordination • Reduced muscle strength	• Decreased attention and alertness • Reduced ability to make rational decisions • Increase in anxiety and depression • Decrease in patience
1–1.5%	• Dramatic slowing of reactions • Poor balance and clumsiness • Difficulty seeing • Slurred speech • Vomiting, especially if this BAC is reached rapidly	• Little awareness of what is happening around you
1.6–2.9%	• Severe motor impairment, e.g. frequently staggering or falling	• Little or no awareness of what is happening around you
3–3.9%	• Loss of consciousness • Anaesthesia (complete loss of feelings/sensations) • Death (for many)	• Non-responsive stupor or coma
Above 4%	• Unconsciousness • Cessation of breathing • Death, usually due to respiratory failure	• Non-responsive stupor or coma

Watch the video on FolensOnline about teenagers drinking alcohol, then discuss the following questions as a class.

1. What risky behaviours do you think teenagers might engage in when they are under the influence of alcohol?

2. The average age for starting to drink is now thought to be 14. Do you think this is accurate or do most teenagers not drink until a later age?

3. Why do you think that teenagers who start drinking at a young age are more likely to become involved in drug abuse?

◼ Low-risk alcohol guidelines for adults ◼

The following low-risk alcohol guidelines are for adults. There is no 'safe' amount of alcohol recommended for teenagers.

* Always eat before drinking alcohol.

* Drinks should be spaced out over the week and should never be saved up to drink all on one occasion.

* Aim for *at least* two alcohol-free days each week. The guidelines (for adults only) are:

* Eleven standard drinks (110 grams pure alcohol) spread out over the week for women, with at least two alcohol-free days

* Seventeen standard drinks (170 grams pure alcohol) spread out over the week for men, with at least two alcohol-free days

* Regularly drinking above the guidelines can cause severe short-term and long-term damage.

* Binge drinking (having six or more standard drinks in one sitting) can significantly increase your risk of developing physical health issues, including liver disease, cancer and high blood pressure. Remember, alcohol is a depressant and can have serious negative effects on your mental health.

Go to the Drinkaware website to find out how many standard drinks are in the following:

- 1 pint of beer/lager or cider: _____
- 1 can of beer/lager or cider: _____
- 1 bottle of beer/lager or cider: _____
- 1 small glass of wine: _____
- 1 bottle of wine: _____
- 1 pub measure of spirits: _____

Unfortunately, Ireland has one of the highest rates of drunkenness among school students, according to the European School Survey. However, this is not only a problem among teenagers. Go to the Alcohol Action Ireland website and you will see some very worrying facts related to alcohol and health among Irish adults on the 'Alcohol Facts' page. Write some of these statistics below.

_____

_____

_____

_____

■ Alcohol and the law ■

It is against the law for a young person under 18 to:

∗ Buy alcohol

∗ Drink alcohol in a public place

∗ Pretend to be over 18 in order to buy alcohol

∗ Be in a pub after 9:00 p.m. from 1 October to 30 April or 10:00 p.m. from 1 May to 30 September

The following are also against the law:

∗ It is against the law for a young person under 15 to be in a pub at all without a parent or guardian.

∗ A young person between 15 and 17 can attend a private function, such as a wedding, in a pub after the times above if a proper meal is being served.

∗ It is also against the law for an adult to buy alcohol for a young person under the age of 18.

∗ In a private residence, alcohol can't be served to a visiting young person (under 18) without the explicit consent of that young person's parent or guardian.

Write a positive message to a teenager who is worried about a parent's problem drinking and doesn't know who to ask for help.

NO ALCOHOL

_____

_____

_____

Rapid recap

3

Topics we discussed today:

1. _____

2. _____

3. _____

2

People or places I could find out more information on this lesson from:

1. _____

2. _____

1

Something in today's lesson that I would like to learn more about:

1. _____

Parent's/guardian's signature _____

(Your teacher will tell you if this should be signed each week.)

Look up the following words in a dictionary and write what they mean.

Stupor: _____

Rational: _____

Inhibitions: _____

Complete your personal learning journal at home.

12. Alcohol and decisions

At the end of this lesson, you will:

Understand the personal and social consequences of alcohol consumption

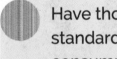

Have thought about personal standards in relation to alcohol consumption

Key words

abc

Inhibition

Personal standards

❤ **Active**

🧠 **Aware**

🐾 **Responsible**

Everybody should stand up and stretch – reach for the ceiling, turn left and right, then touch your toes. (If you can't do this, you can improvise with a stretch you can do.) Take three deep breaths all the way down to your belly. Finally, complete this sentence: I am happy because...

Alcohol – your decision

You have to make a decision about your life and your alcohol consumption. Your family, friends and peers may or may not drink alcohol, but you have to make up your own mind. You need to realise that any decision you make regarding alcohol can have a huge impact on your mental health, your sexual health and your life.

Alcohol and your mental health

Drinking alcohol can affect your decision-making and your mental health. The My World Survey captured the views of almost 14,500 people aged 12 to 25 years in Ireland. It found that:

* Depression and anxiety were significantly higher when a young person engaged in harmful drinking.

* There is clear evidence that excessive use of alcohol is associated with poor mental health and wellbeing.

* For young adults, strong links were found between excessive drinking and suicidal behaviour.

Alcohol and your sexual health

The parts of the brain responsible for impulse control don't fully mature until you are about age 25. This means teenagers are more likely to make impulsive, emotional decisions without thinking about the consequences.

* When a teenager drinks alcohol, inhibitions are lowered, impulsiveness increases and decision-making gets worse.

* Teenagers are more likely to have unplanned sexual activity if they are drunk and are less likely to use contraception or use it safely. This increases their risk of getting sexually transmitted infections (STIs) and an unplanned pregnancy.

Inhibition

abc

A feeling that makes you self-conscious and more reserved.

* Drunken people often behave in embarrassing ways, saying or doing things that they later regret. For a young person, this can have a huge negative effect on their self-confidence and their reputation and can lead to further drinking to try to forget what they have done.

Alcohol and your life

* Choosing to drink at an early age increases a person's chances of developing problems with alcohol use in later life.

* Alcohol affects the developing adolescent brain in a different way than it does the adult brain. During adolescence, alcohol use can damage two key parts of the brain: the area responsible for logic, reasoning, self-regulation and judgement as well as an area of the brain related to learning and memory.

* Alcohol is very high in calories and can cause weight gain.

* Drinking alcohol can affect academic and sporting achievement, as it can do permanent damage to brain development, thinking skills and memory. It can also greatly reduce fitness levels.

* Being hung over or tired from drinking alcohol will affect your learning in school and create a bad impression.

* Co-ordination and reaction time slow down with alcohol consumption. This, combined with lowered inhibitions, greatly increases the risk of accidents.

■ Setting standards in relation to alcohol ■

Some people choose to never drink alcohol for various reasons. Some people choose to drink alcohol very rarely. Some choose to join groups such as the Pioneer Association, a group committed to bringing public attention to the ill effects of excessive use of alcohol and drugs in Ireland, and pledge to never drink. Some young people choose to take a pledge to not drink alcohol until they are 18.

Personal standards are a set of behaviours built on expectations you have for yourself.

For homework you will be asked to set some personal standards for yourself in relation to drinking alcohol. (You won't need to share what you write.) Examples of personal standards in relation to alcohol consumption could be to promise yourself that you will not drink until you are 18 years old, that you will never drink more than three drinks in one night or that you will only ever drink at a special occasion in the company of your parents.

List some reasons why a person may choose not to drink alcohol.

_____

_____

_____

Watch Áine's story on FolensOnline, in which she discusses her latest dilemma, then answer the following questions as a class.

1. What personal standards had Áine set for herself in relation to drinking alcohol? What were her reasons?

_____

_____

_____

2. Why is she now considering drinking?

_____

_____

_____

Watch Mark's story on FolensOnline, then answer the following questions.

1. Why did Mark get drunk?

_____

_____

_____

_____

2. Had Mark set personal standards for himself in relation to alcohol?

_____

_____

_____

3. Did drinking help him cope with his problems?

_____

_____

_____

4. How does he feel after his drunken behaviour?

_____

_____

_____

Write a positive message to Joe, whose friends keep making fun of him for not drinking. He doesn't drink because he doesn't want to, but now he is thinking he might try it just to make them happy.

_____

_____

_____

Rapid recap

3

Topics we discussed today:

1. _____

2. _____

3. _____

2

People or places I could find out more information on this lesson from:

1. _____

2. _____

1

Something in today's lesson that I would like to learn more about:

1. _____

Parent's/guardian's signature _____

(Your teacher will tell you if this should be signed each week.)

In your personal learning journal, write two personal standards for yourself in relation to alcohol consumption.

Complete your personal learning journal at home.

13. Substance use

At the end of this lesson, you will:

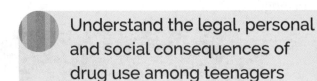 Understand the legal, personal and social consequences of drug use among teenagers

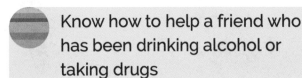 Know how to help a friend who has been drinking alcohol or taking drugs

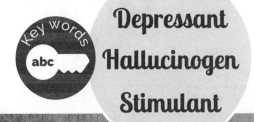 Know where to get help with drug-related issues

Key words

abc

Depressant
Hallucinogen
Stimulant

DRUGS

💡 Aware
🌱 Resilient
🏃 Responsible

In pairs, unscramble the following words. All are names of drugs. It is a race to see which pair finishes first.

lohcoal _____

hinore _____

binscana _____

steascy _____

fineefac _____

The effects of drugs

Drugs can affect people differently. Some drugs will cause you to have lots of energy (uppers or stimulants). Others can cause you to relax (downers or depressants). Some can cause you to see and hear things differently (hallucinogens).

Write the names of the drugs listed below in the table according to whether you think they are uppers, downers or hallucinogens. You can find this information on the Drugs.ie website.

alcohol   ketamine

amphetamine   LSD

caffeine   magic mushrooms

cannabis   methadone

cocaine   methamphetamine

ecstasy   nicotine

heroin

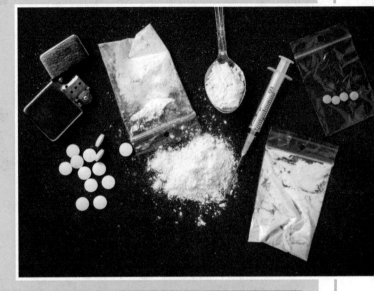

Uppers (stimulants)	Downers (depressants)	Hallucinogens

How can I encourage my friend to stop taking drugs?

* Try to talk to your friend and listen to what they have to say.

* Go online to find out more about the drugs they are using. Tell your friend about the risks and let them know that you are worried about them.

* Try to keep your friend away from situations where people may be using drugs by suggesting alternative places to go together.

* Let them know that you are there for them. Find out about local services where they can get help and advice. You can find this information online on the Drugs.ie website and you can search by your county.

My parent has a drug problem, how can I get help?

* If you can't talk to your parent and encourage them to get help, talk to another adult, family member, friend or teacher.

* If your parent or carer is using drugs and it is causing problems at home, it can be very upsetting and worrying. However, your parent's problem should not become your problem.

* Read the Teenhelp section on parental drug and alcohol problems on the Barnardos website, call Childline on 1800 66 66 66 or text Talk to 50101.

Do you think there are many services in Ireland to help people who suffer from drug or alcohol addiction? Do you think there are many services to support their families?

Drugs and the law

It is illegal to grow drugs such as cannabis or to be in possession of illegal drugs. If the Gardaí have reason to suspect you have drugs, they have the power to search you (and your vehicle). However, you have the right to:

* Ask why you have been stopped

* At the end of the search, ask for a record of the search

* Ask to see the Garda's warrant card if they are not in uniform

* Not be detained if you are under 18 without your parents or carers being contacted

* If you are found in possession of drugs, the court must decide if it was intended for personal use or to supply others

Have there been any recent cases in the media in relation to drugs?

■ Stay safe advice for teenagers

Unlike adults, there are no low-risk guidelines for teenagers' alcohol consumption, as it is not safe for teenagers to drink any alcohol at all. There are no low-risk guidelines for drugs either. The only way to safely take drugs is as prescribed by a doctor or pharmacist. However, if your friend has been drinking alcohol or taking drugs, follow these guidelines:

* Don't let him or her separate from you or your friends.

* Don't let a friend go home alone or go off with a stranger.

* Don't provoke a fight by arguing with or laughing at someone who is drunk.

* Don't give a drunk person a cold shower, as the shock might make them pass out.

* For sobering up, there is no substitute for time. It takes as many hours as the number of units drunk to sober up. In other words, it takes one hour for one unit of alcohol to leave your system.

Can you think of any more advice?

■ What to do if there is an emergency with someone who is using drugs or drinking alcohol

* If someone passes out, ring 112 and ask for an ambulance.

* Don't leave them alone.

* Turn the person on their side into the recovery position so that they can breathe freely and will not swallow vomit if they get sick.

* When the ambulance arrives, tell the paramedics anything you know about the drugs or alcohol they used. Don't lie to save your friend from getting in trouble – telling the truth could save their life.

In groups, make posters or leaflets for students in your school with the slogan 'Think before you drink' or 'Get high on life, not drugs'.

Write a positive message to Linda, who is worried about her mother's drug and alcohol problem but is afraid to call Childline in case they try to take Linda away from her mother.

_____

_____

_____

Rapid recap

3

Topics we discussed today:

1._____

2._____

3._____

2

People or places I could find out more information on this lesson from:

1._____

2._____

1

Something in today's lesson that I would like to learn more about:

1._____

Parent's/guardian's signature _____

(Your teacher will tell you if this should be signed each week.)

Go to the SpunOut website and find three ways drug use affects one's mental health. Write them below.

_____

_____

_____

Complete your personal learning journal at home.

Strand review

In this strand, you learned about:

- Eating well
- Staying well
- Dealing with conflict and criticism
- Roles and responsibilities at home
- Taking care online
- Alcohol
- Alcohol and decisions
- Substance use

Look back over the lessons that you completed. In the table below, tick the skills that you think you learned or used.

Managing myself

- I know myself better. ◯
- I made decisions. ◯
- I set goals. ◯
- I achieved goals. ◯
- I thought about what I learned. ◯
- I used technology to learn. ◯

Staying well

- I am healthy and active. ◯
- I am social. ◯
- I feel safe. ◯
- I am spiritual. ◯
- I feel confident. ◯
- I feel positive about what I learned. ◯

Communicating

- I used language. ◯
- I used numbers. ◯
- I listened to my classmates. ◯
- I expressed myself. ◯
- I performed/ presented. ◯
- I had a discussion/ debate. ◯
- I used technology to communicate. ◯

Being literate

- I understand some new words. ◯
- I enjoyed words and language. ◯
- I wrote for different reasons. ◯
- I expressed my ideas clearly. ◯
- I developed my spoken language. ◯
- I read and wrote in different ways. ◯

Being creative

- I used my imagination. ◯
- I thought about things from a different point of view. ◯
- I put ideas into action. ◯
- I learned in a creative way. ◯
- I was creative with digital technology. ◯

Working with others

- I developed relationships. ◯
- I dealt with conflict. ◯
- I co-operated. ◯
- I respected difference. ◯
- I helped make the world a better place. ◯
- I learned with others. ◯
- I worked with others using digital technology. ◯

Managing information and thinking

- I was curious. ◯
- I gathered and analysed information. ◯
- I thought creatively. ◯
- I thought about what I learned. ◯
- I used digital technology to access, manage and share information. ◯

Being numerate

- I expressed ideas mathematically. ◯
- I estimated, predicted and calculated. ◯
- I was interested in problem-solving. ◯
- I saw patterns and trends. ◯
- I gathered and presented data. ◯
- I used digital technology to review and understand numbers. ◯

Now write two skills from the list that you think you should focus on more in the future.

_____

_____

Team up

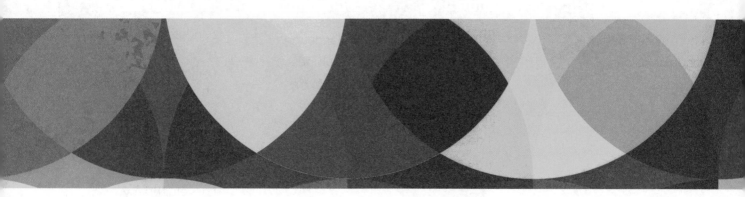

This strand focuses on learning about important relationships in your life and building relationship skills.

Strand learning outcomes

- Evaluate attitudes, skills and values that help to make, maintain and end friendships

- Explain the different influences on relationships and levels of intimacy

- Analyse relationship difficulties experienced by young people

- Describe fertility, conception, pre-natal development and birth, and the particular health considerations for each

- Explain what it means to take care of your sexual health

- Demonstrate assertive communication skills in support of responsible, informed decision-making about relationships and sexual health that are age and developmentally appropriate

- Reflect on the personal and social dimensions of sexual orientation and gender identity

- Critically analyse the use of sexual imagery and gender stereotyping in various forms of media

- Critique the influence of media on your understanding of sexuality and sexual health

14. Body image

At the end of this lesson, you will:

 Have examined the ideal media body image for males and females

 Understand how media images may be enhanced

 Have reflected on the influence of the media on your body image

 Appreciate unique qualities in others and in yourself

Key words
abc

Body image

Conventional

Be**you**tiful

🧠 **Aware**

🤲 **Connected**

As a class, pick four celebrities (two male, two female) who are considered to be a conventional beauty. Look at their images online and list some of the characteristics that they have that are considered beautiful.

abc **Conventional** means a socially accepted style or idea.

abc Your **body image** is your own view of how you see yourself.

Body image and the media

We sometimes look at magazines and think 'I wish I had perfect skin like her' or 'I wish I had big muscles like him', but these images are often unrealistic.

Body image is influenced by your self-esteem, your emotions, what people say about you and by the media. Some people don't realise that most of the photos we see in magazines are retouched or airbrushed to make the models or celebrities look better. This can impact hugely on our own body image, as it can make us feel inadequate and inferior because we don't look like that.

Watch the video about airbrushing on FolensOnline.

1. Now that you've looked at the photos and the video, work in groups to list the changes that are often made to improve the appearance of photos in magazines.

_____

_____

2. In the table below, write some standards or 'norms' that are set by the media regarding beauty. In the right-hand column, list some of the things that people do to try to achieve this. One example has been done for you.

Media standard	What people do to achieve this
Women should be thin	Crash diets, slimming pills

1. In pairs, write an email in your copy to your favourite magazine expressing your opinion about airbrushing.

2. Society has a set idea of what is beautiful and what is not. This is strongly influenced by the media. Using the internet, find images of people who are considered beautiful. Make a collage of all your images with the title 'Media's image of beauty'. Discuss each picture and examine how realistic or attainable that image is.

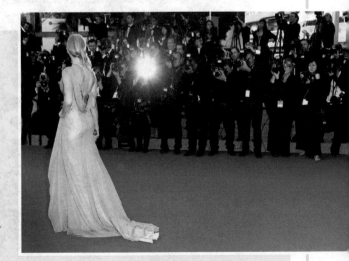

Improving your body image

Body image is a huge part of teenagers' lives. Teenagers are often judged on how they look, especially on social media through likes or comments.

It's important to remember that nobody is totally happy with how they look, but you can take steps to feel more comfortable with your body image. For example, exercising is good for your body and your mind. Taking care of your personal hygiene will also help. You can build your self-esteem through positive thinking and by realising how special you are.

For homework, you will be asked to do an exercise that can help you to improve your body image. You don't need to share your answers. Improving your body image is not an instant thing. Like self-esteem, it is something you have to be aware of and try to improve over time by being realistic and accepting the things that you can't change.

Prejudice and physical appearance

Beautiful people can be kind, caring, smart and funny, just like a person who is not considered to be conventionally beautiful. Don't stereotype or prejudge people just because of how they look. Beauty is superficial. It is only the surface of that person – it does not tell you about their character, their strengths, their weaknesses and their unique qualities.

Any age group can choose or dismiss a boyfriend or girlfriend based on how they look, but adolescents in particular are more focused on how people look instead of how they act and their unique qualities.

1. Consider the following:

   ● If your parent was very sick and you wanted to talk to someone, would you choose to talk to someone because they are (a) beautiful or (b) kind?

   ● If you wanted someone to make you laugh, would you choose someone because they are (a) beautiful or (b) funny?

   ● If you were going to be holding hands with someone on the front page of a magazine, would you choose someone because they are (a) smart or (b) beautiful?

   ● If you were really stressed about exams, would you choose to relax with someone because they are (a) beautiful or (b) calming and caring?

2. List three of your unique qualities.

   _____

   _____

   _____

3. Silently reflect on how many times each day you judge someone else's size or appearance (for example, a peer, a stranger, a friend, a family member or a teacher).

1. How can we avoid judging others based on physical appearance?

2. If you were looking for a romantic partner right now, how important would looks be over personality?

3. How important would looks or physical appearance be to you in a relationship in 20 or 40 years' time?

Assessment idea

Design a resource for your peers called 'Improving Your Body Image'. Include practical tips as well as advice on improving self-esteem and positive thinking.

Write a positive message to Lara, who is upset because she heard her aunt describing her looks as quirky and unusual.

_____

_____

_____

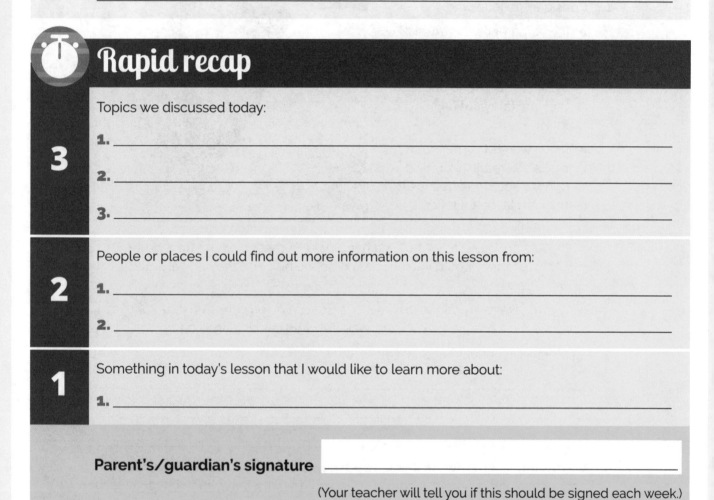

Rapid recap

3

Topics we discussed today:

1. _____

2. _____

3. _____

2

People or places I could find out more information on this lesson from:

1. _____

2. _____

1

Something in today's lesson that I would like to learn more about:

1. _____

Parent's/guardian's signature _____

(Your teacher will tell you if this should be signed each week.)

Complete the following in your personal learning journal. You don't have to share your answers with anyone.

1. List at least two physical features that you like about yourself.

2. List two things about your body that make you different from everybody else.

3. List one thing about your body that you don't like but can't change.

4. List one thing about your body that you don't like that you *can* change by yourself. (Maybe there is no part that you don't like, and that is great!)

Complete your personal learning journal at home.

15. Respect in relationships

At the end of this lesson, you will:

 Understand the importance of respect in a relationship

 Recognise an unhealthy relationship

 Know how to help a friend in an unhealthy relationship

 Key words
abc

Respect
Responsibility
Right

 Aware
 Respected
 Responsible

In groups, write one of the letters from the word RESPECT on an A4 page (your teacher will assign you a letter). Decorate each letter with words, pictures, sayings and symbols that you associate with respect in a romantic relationship. Put all the letters together to display in your classroom.

Respect in relationships

Last year you learned about rights and responsibilities in relationships. You need to be aware of your rights and responsibilities in romantic relationships and you need to respect your partner's rights.

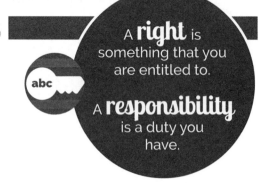

A **right** is something that you are entitled to.

A **responsibility** is a duty you have.

My Life 2, Lesson 19

In pairs, discuss each of the following guidelines on how you can show respect to a romantic partner. Give one example of how you can show respect in each instance.

1. Respect their personal beliefs, values and religion:

   _____

2. Respect their choices about sex:

   _____

3. Show respect to their families:

   _____

4. Don't pressure them to do things they don't want to do:

   _____

5. Respect their right to privacy:

   _____

   _____

   _____

   _____

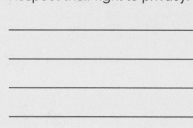

Watch Joe's story on FolensOnline, in which he talks about religion and dating.

1. How was Mary disrespectful to Joe?

   _____

   _____

   _____

2. How did Joe feel?

   _____

3. What should he do?

   _____

4. Do you think teenagers consider religion when dating someone?

   _____

Unhealthy relationships

Being in a relationship should make a person feel respected, happy, safe and loved. However, some people find themselves in unhealthy or abusive relationships and may find it difficult to leave or end the relationship. Below are some examples of disrespectful behaviour and abuse that can cause an unhealthy relationship.

Physical abuse

Physical abuse is the intentional use of force or threats of force. It can include hitting, shoving, punching, kicking or throwing things. It is a common misconception that relationship violence only happens to older married women with children. This is not the case. In a national survey on domestic violence, almost 60% of those who had experienced severe abuse in intimate relationships first experienced it when they were under the age of 25.

Verbal abuse

Verbal abuse consists of shouting, screaming, name-calling or insults.

Emotional abuse

Emotional abuse can include spreading rumours, lying, possessiveness or attacking a person's self-esteem by telling them they are useless or stupid. It may also include their mobile phone calls, texts and social media being monitored. It can involve manipulation or mind games.

Sexual abuse

Sexual abuse occurs when someone forces any form of sexual activity on someone else without that person's consent.

 Discuss possible reasons why a teenager might stay in an abusive relationship and not tell anyone what is happening.

How to help

What should you do if you think your friend is in an abusive relationship?

* **Listen** to what your friend has to say.

* **Tell your friend that they are not to blame.** Remind your friend that it is the partner who is choosing this behaviour.

* **Offer support.** If your friend chooses not to end the relationship, you should keep supporting them. Do this by listening, talking and challenging your friend to think about what to do. Continue to be a friend even when you feel frustrated by their decisions or actions.

* **Mention other people your friend might talk to.** This could include a counsellor, a teacher, another adult they trust or a help agency. Find out more about abusive relationships and how to get help in the Teenhelp section on the Barnardos website.

 Watch Deirdre and Pete's story on FolensOnline. Imagine you are Deirdre's friend and you are getting ready to talk to Deirdre about her relationship.

1. How would you bring up the subject?

_____

_____

2. What main concerns would you have for Deirdre?

_____

3. In your opinion, what needs to change in the relationship?

_____

4. Should the relationship continue?

_____

5. Where would you tell Deirdre that she can get more help and advice?

_____

Write a positive message to Nicola, who is worried that her friend is in an unhealthy relationship but doesn't want to embarrass him by mentioning it.

_____

_____

_____

Rapid recap

Topics we discussed today:

3

1. _____

2. _____

3. _____

People or places I could find out more information on this lesson from:

2

1. _____

2. _____

Something in today's lesson that I would like to learn more about:

1

1. _____

Parent's/guardian's signature _____

(Your teacher will tell you if this should be signed each week.)

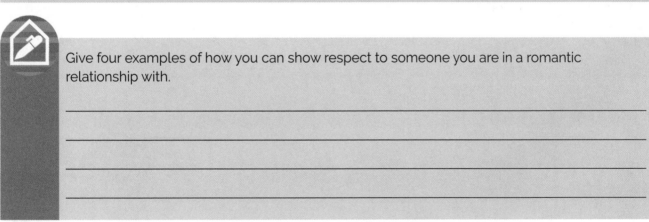

Give four examples of how you can show respect to someone you are in a romantic relationship with.

_____

_____

_____

_____

Complete your personal learning journal at home.

16. Setting boundaries in relationships

At the end of this lesson, you will:

 Have examined the advantages of abstinence or delaying first sex

Know how to communicate your decision to a partner

 Key words

Abstinence

Age of consent

Boundary

Virgin

🧠 **Aware**
🌱 **Resilient**
🤝 **Respected**
✊ **Responsible**

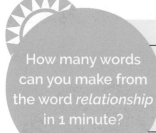

How many words can you make from the word *relationship* in 1 minute?

Setting boundaries

In a healthy relationship, both partners should be able to express their feelings and respect each other's boundaries about sex. You shouldn't have to have sex to keep your partner happy. You may feel comfortable kissing or touching, and that is okay. You should set your own boundaries regarding sexual activity and have relationships with people who respect your boundaries. An example of a boundary regarding sexual activity is delaying or postponing sex until a certain age or until you are with a person for a certain amount of time. There are many reasons why young people will choose to delay the age at which they first have sex.

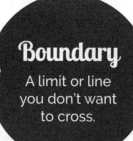

abc

Boundary
A limit or line you don't want to cross.

Early sex

You learned last year that the age of consent in Ireland for sexual intercourse is 17. Most teenagers are over 17 when they first have sex. However, some teenagers choose to have a sexual relationship before this age.

Having sex with the right person can be wonderful, but while teenagers are physically able to have a sexual relationship, they often are not mature enough to deal with the emotions, responsibilities and consequences that come with a sexual relationship. For example, along with the risk of an unplanned pregnancy, there is also the risk of catching a sexually transmitted infection (STI).

My Life 2, Lesson 19

Age of consent

The age at which a person is considered to be legally able to consent to sexual activity.

Discuss the following research undertaken by the Crisis Pregnancy Programme on 7,441 young Irish people. Discuss the reasons for each statistic. Are you surprised by any of them?

- Boys and girls who had sex under the age of 17 were twice as likely to get a sexually transmitted infection (STI) in their lifetime.

- Young people who have sex before the age of 17 are less likely to use contraception.

- Boys and girls who had sex under the age of 17 were more likely to say that they regretted it and that they were not in love with the person.

- Boys and girls who had sex under the age of 17 were also more likely to say that they never had sex with that person again.

- Girls who had sex under the age of 17 were over 70% more likely to have a crisis pregnancy in their lifetime.

Abstinence

Abstinence can mean different things to different people. For some, it means no intimate touching with other people. For others it could mean some intimate touching, but not sexual intercourse. Remember that pregnancy can occur without intercourse if sperm is ejaculated near the entrance of the vagina or on an area that comes into contact with the vagina. STIs such as herpes and genital warts can be passed through skin-to-skin genital contact.

A person who is abstinent is not necessarily a virgin. Someone who is abstinent may have had sexual intercourse in the past, but is not currently sexually active. Just because a person has had sex before does not mean that that person must feel pressured to have sex again. Your partner has the right to choose abstinence and you should respect their choice if they do. If you don't want to have sex, you need to communicate this clearly to your partner.

abc *Abstinence* means choosing not to have sexual activity.

abc *Virgin* Someone who has never had sexual intercourse.

In groups, discuss and give examples of reasons why a young person would choose abstinence or to not have sex at an early age. One example has already done for you in each category below.

Personal reasons:

Personal values or religious/moral beliefs

Medical reasons:

Fear of pregnancy

Relational reasons:

Haven't met the right person

Qualities that will help maintain abstinence or delay sexual activity

* Ability to resist pressure
* Respect for other person's feelings
* Good self-esteem
* High degree of self-control
* Ability to communicate well – can say 'no' in an assertive way

Reasons that a commitment to be abstinent or postpone sexual activity might fail

* Fear of saying no
* Pressure from your partner
* Peer pressure – 'everyone is doing it'
* Wanting to be loved
* Low self-esteem
* Using alcohol or drugs

Communicating your decision

If you are choosing abstinence or don't want to have sex yet, you must clearly communicate this to your partner. If you *are* choosing to have sex, you should communicate to your partner the boundaries you have set if they are asking you to do something that you are not comfortable with.

Use verbal communication

* Say 'no'.
* Tell your partner you want to stay abstinent or not have sex yet or that you aren't comfortable with this.

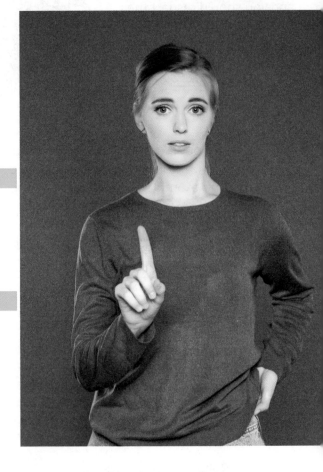

Use body language

* Use serious facial expressions.
* Create distance between you and your partner.
* Cross your arms.
* Stop touching or kissing.
* Look them in the eye.

Use delay tactics

* Stop kissing or touching.
* Tell your partner you have to call home or be somewhere.
* Say you need to get a drink of water.

Suggest alternatives

* Ask a group of friends to go out together.

* Go to a movie.

* Suggest playing a sport or another activity.

Build the relationship

* Explain your feelings.

* Make sure your partner knows that you made a decision to stay abstinent before this moment and that it is something you feel strongly about.

 Watch Lisa's story on FolensOnline, in which she talks about having sex for the first time. In groups, answer the questions below.

1. How do you think Lisa feels in this situation?

   _____

   _____

   _____

   _____

   _____

2. What do you think about what Jack did?

   _____

   _____

   _____

   _____

3. What should Lisa do now?

   _____

   _____

   _____

   _____

Aoife told her boyfriend that she was ready to have sex. Now she has changed her mind. She doesn't want him to think she is a liar and she doesn't want him to break up with her, but she doesn't know what she will say to him. What advice would you give to Aoife?

_____

_____

_____

Rapid recap

3

Topics we discussed today:

1. _____

2. _____

3. _____

2

People or places I could find out more information on this lesson from:

1. _____

2. _____

1

Something in today's lesson that I would like to learn more about:

1. _____

Parent's/guardian's signature _____

(Your teacher will tell you if this should be signed each week.)

Watch the videos on the B4UDecide website that discuss early sex, saying no to sex and peer pressure.

Complete your personal learning journal at home.

17. Sexual health

At the end of this lesson, you will:

Be aware of your sexual health

Have analysed how the media can influence your understanding of sexual health and sexuality

Key words
abc

Fertility
Sexually
transmitted
infection
(STI)

💡 **Aware**
🤲 **Connected**
🙌 **Responsible**

Play a game of charades. One student acts out the title of a movie and the class has to guess what it is. As today's lesson is about sexual health, choose a movie that has a love story or romance in it.

Sexual imagery in the media

We are bombarded with sexual imagery in the media. We are constantly exposed to provocative sexual images on social media, on TV and in magazines. For example, it has become the norm for singers or actors in music videos to wear very little or very suggestive clothing.

There is growing concern about young people's exposure to sexual content in the media and about its effects on their sexual health, attitudes, beliefs and behaviours. Although sexual content in the media can affect any age group, adolescents may be particularly vulnerable, as you are still learning and developing your gender roles, sexual attitudes and sexual behaviours. In the media we are usually presented with a positive, fun image of sex, but very little is said about the potential risks and consequences. These messages are not a true indication of real life or real relationships.

Do you agree that we are bombarded with sexual imagery in the media? (Watch an older music video for contrast.) Do you think these images and messages have any impact on your life and your ideas about sex and relationships?

Fertility

Teenage boys and girls are extremely fertile. But being physically capable of having a baby does not mean that a person is emotionally ready to cope with having a child. For women, fertility decreases with age. Men remain fertile for most of their lives. Fertility for both sexes can be damaged by excessive dieting, smoking cigarettes or cannabis and contracting some STIs. This may not be a big deal to you now, but as you get older and may want to start a family, fertility will be extremely important.

Fertility is the ability to have children.

The HPV vaccine

The HPV vaccine is a vaccine against human papilloma virus (HPV). The vaccine protects against the two strains of HPV that cause cervical cancer in over 70% of women. It does *not* protect against any other sexually transmitted infections or against pregnancy. The vaccine is given to young teenage girls as three injections given at intervals.

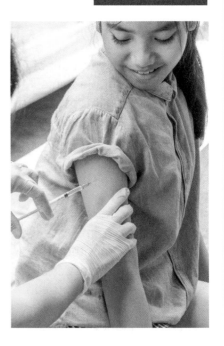

Testicular cancer

Boys should examine their testicles once a month. This involves holding the testicle between the thumb and the index and middle finger and rolling gently to feel for lumps. If you do feel a lump that you think is different, go to your doctor for advice. Testicular cancer is very treatable, especially if caught early. Find out more on how to check and other symptoms on the Irish Cancer Society website.

Breast cancer

Every woman needs to be breast aware. (Men can get breast cancer too, but it is much less common.) The sooner you notice a change, the better, because if cancer is found early, treatment is more likely to be successful. Girls should develop a habit of checking their breasts once a month to see if there are any changes. Find out how to complete a breast exam on the Irish Cancer Society website.

Do you hear much about breast cancer, cervical cancer or testicular cancer in the media? Do you think teenagers are well educated on these topics?

■ Bodybuilding supplements ■

There are a huge amount of bodybuilding supplements available, so it is impossible to say what is safe and what is not. However, any supplement containing steroids can cause harm, in particular to teenagers. They increase the level of hormones in the body, and in extreme cases this can cause impotence and loss of sex drive. Certain additives in supplements can be dangerous to body organs, such as the kidneys.

 List three ways that you can take care of your sexual health.

_____

_____

_____

■ Sexually transmitted infections ■

STIs are passed on during sex. They are caused by specific bacteria and viruses. Kissing and touching each other's genitals may pass on some STIs. The most common STIs in Ireland are genital warts, genital herpes and chlamydia.

The only sure way to avoid getting a sexually transmitted infection is by avoiding any intimate touching with a partner. In an intimate relationship, you can reduce your risk by:

SEXUAL HEALTH

* Using condoms

* Limiting the number of partners you have – the more partners you have, the greater your chance of coming into contact with an infected person

* Talking to your partner about STIs and practising safer sex

To find out more about this topic, go to the B4UDecide website.

Sexually transmitted infection (STI)
An infection that is passed on from an infected partner through sexual activity.

How would I know I have an STI?

You might not know if you have an STI. Some STIs have no symptoms, so you can't tell if you or your partner is infected. If you are sexually active, it is important to have regular check-ups.

Some STIs can cause long-term problems if left untreated, such as infertility, complications in pregnancy and pelvic inflammatory disease.

You should go to your GP or an STI clinic if you are worried about STIs or are sexually active and notice any of the following symptoms:

* Unusual discharge from the penis or vagina

* Pain when passing urine

* Unusual sores or blisters in the genital area

* Itching or irritation in the genital area

* Pain during sex

Once diagnosed, most STIs can be cured with medication. Some STIs can only be treated to reduce symptoms but will stay in your system and may reoccur.

STI facts

* You may not know if you have an STI.

* You may not be able to tell if your partner has an STI.

* You can get an STI the first time or any time you have sex.

* You can catch an STI more than once.

* You can be infected with more than one STI at a time.

* STIs can be passed on through oral sex.

1. In groups, discuss some of the emotions that might arise from a sexual relationship and list them below.

   _____

   _____

2. List some possible consequences of teenagers having a sexual relationship.

   _____

   _____

3. What responsibilities do teenagers in a sexual relationship have?

   _____

   _____

Write a positive message to Anthony, who has a question about sexual health but is too embarrassed to ask anyone in case they laugh at him.

_____

_____

_____

Rapid recap

3

Topics we discussed today:

1. _____

2. _____

3. _____

2

People or places I could find out more information on this lesson from:

1. _____

2. _____

1

Something in today's lesson that I would like to learn more about:

1. _____

Parent's/guardian's signature _____

(Your teacher will tell you if this should be signed each week.)

Take the pregnancy and STI quiz on the B4UDecide website.

Complete your personal learning journal at home.

18. Relationship problems

At the end of this lesson, you will:

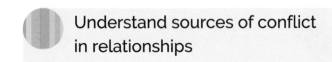
Understand sources of conflict in relationships

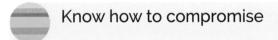
Know how to compromise

Key words
abc Compromise

🤲 **Connected**
🤝 **Respected**

In groups, complete the following task. Imagine that an alien has landed on Earth. The alien is from the planet Ukatron, where there is no such thing as gender. You have been chosen to explain the differences between males and females to the alien. In your copy, write the speech that you will present to the alien so that it can report back to its planet about the males and females on Earth.

People say 'men are from Mars and women are from Venus', but what does that mean? Do you think gay relationships have less conflict, as the people are the same gender and so might understand each other better? Can boys and girls just be friends or does someone always have a romantic intention?

Imagine that you are holding interviews to find the perfect romantic partner. Make a list of five questions that you would ask the candidates to help you decide.

_____

_____

_____

_____

_____

_____

_____

Relationship conflict

There is no such thing as a relationship without conflict, be it a relationship with a friend, a family member or a boyfriend or girlfriend. Conflict is a part of life and exists in every relationship. Conflict is not necessarily bad – sometimes it can lead to a deeper understanding or coming together to work out problems. However, how the conflict is resolved can determine whether a relationship will be healthy or unhealthy.

Sources of conflict

Below is a list of possible sources of conflict in relationships. Read the list and add more to it.

* Money

* Sex/intimacy

* Religion

* Wants

* Politics

* Beliefs/values

* Personal flaws or addiction (such as drinking, smoking or gambling)

* Distrust (such as dishonesty or jealousy)

* Lack of time together (due to work or study)

* _____

* _____

* _____

In the table below, list some of the most common sources of conflict in each of your relationships. Use the above list to help you, but feel free to add other sources of conflict (don't use names).

Friends, boyfriends/girlfriends	Family

Learning how to compromise

One way to resolve conflict in a relationship is to compromise. Compromising is not always easy, as you can sometimes feel like you are losing or giving in if you don't stand your ground. However, a compromise is a settlement that can make everyone happy. It involves negotiation and give and take from everyone involved. Follow these guidelines for reaching a compromise.

* **Listen to the other person's opinion.** Let the other person explain to you why they feel a certain way or want a specific thing.

* **Clearly state why you feel as you do.** You must calmly explain why you have strong feelings about whatever you are conflicted about so that the other person knows where you are coming from.

* **Be open to suggestions.** Don't refuse to change your mind. Remember, you're not always right.

* **Don't try to win.** Being in a relationship is not about winning or getting your own way. Reaching a compromise is about deciding something that will make you both happy.

* **Give a little.** You'll never reach a compromise if you don't give a little. And it shouldn't always be the same person who gives a little – it is up to both of you to do this.

Practise your compromising skills by completing the following activity.

Your group has been asked to decide on four luxury items that the group can bring to a desert island (with no electricity) that you will be living on for four weeks. Each person in the group should write down two items that they would like to bring. The group must decide which four items would be best to bring.

_____

_____

_____

_____

_____

_____

Write a positive message to Andrew, who feels that he is always losing the arguments in his relationship and doesn't know how to get his way.

_____

_____

_____

Rapid recap

3 Topics we discussed today:

1. _____

2. _____

3. _____

2 People or places I could find out more information on this lesson from:

1. _____

2. _____

1 Something in today's lesson that I would like to learn more about:

1. _____

Parent's/guardian's signature _____

(Your teacher will tell you if this should be signed each week.)

Name two people in your life that you would talk to if you experienced conflict in a relationship.

_____

_____

Complete your personal learning journal at home.

19. Responsibilities of pregnancy and parenting

At the end of this lesson, you will:

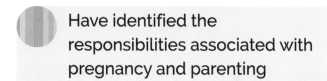 Have identified the responsibilities associated with pregnancy and parenting

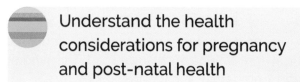 Understand the health considerations for pregnancy and post-natal health

 Recognise the importance of using abstinence or a birth control method to prevent pregnancy

Key words
abc **Contraception**

🌍 **Connected**
👫 **Responsible**

Write a limerick about yourself. The first line should be, 'There once was a girl/boy from …' Read your limerick to the class or the person beside you. Use appropriate language and try to include some truth about yourself.
Here is an example:

There once was a lady from Cork
Whose dad made a living from pork.
He bought for his daughter
A tutor who taught her
To stand on one foot
like a stork.

Teenage pregnancy

Last year you learned about conception, pregnancy and birth. The first step towards a pregnancy should be the parents making a decision to have a child. This is a huge decision and the parents need to understand the day-to-day responsibilities and financial implications of raising a child. They should discuss whether they will have any support from family and friends. Taking care of a baby is hard for anyone, regardless of their age.

My Life 2, Lesson 20

Every year in Ireland, over a thousand teenage girls have babies (there are no figures for the number of teenage boys who become parents, but it is probably quite similar). A baby is a very real and serious consequence of having sexual intercourse. Both parents are equally responsible for raising their child and are responsible for supporting this child until they are an adult. Unfortunately, a teenage mother is more likely to raise a child on her own. Teenage parents may have a more difficult time with money, parenting skills and future job and educational plans.

abc **Contraception**
A method or device used to prevent pregnancy.

Many factors can reduce the chances of becoming a teenage parent, including having goals you don't want to give up, talking with your parents, resisting peer pressure, abstaining from sex or using contraception if you do have sex. The only sure way to avoid pregnancy is to abstain from sex. If you are in an intimate relationship, pregnancy can be prevented if contraception is used properly. Often teenagers don't use contraception properly because they are embarrassed or careless.

The most common types of contraception used by young people are condoms and the oral contraceptive pill. The contraceptive pill does not prevent STIs. To find out more about these and other types of contraception for young people, go to the Think Contraception website.

Do you remember the answers to the following questions from First and Second Year?

- How often is an egg released from the fallopian tubes?_____
- What is the liquid called that sperm travels in?_____
- How long does a pregnancy last?_____
- How does the embryo receive nutrients and oxygen? _____

Pre-natal health

Pregnant mothers have a responsibility to the developing baby, so they must take extra care of themselves to support the development of the baby. They must try to be healthy to avoid any complications during pregnancy.

Go to the HSE website and find out what foods a pregnant woman should be eating plenty of and what foods and lifestyle habits a pregnant woman must avoid.

Home Economics

Eat plenty of	Avoid

Post-natal health

The impact of pregnancy on the health of teenagers and their children can be significant, as many teenagers can be ill-prepared physically, emotionally and socially for pregnancy and parenthood.

Any woman, regardless of age, can suffer from mental ill-health after having a baby. They can develop an illness such as post-natal depression. Post-natal depression (PND) is a type of depression that some women experience after they have had a baby (sometimes men get PND too). There are many symptoms of PND, such as low mood, feeling unable to cope and difficulty sleeping. Many studies show that teenage mothers are more likely to suffer from PND.

Having a baby as a teenager can increase stress and anxiety levels. Being a parent can also affect relationships, as the parents may now have different priorities, responsibilities and attitudes. Combined with lack of sleep, this can all lead to conflict.

Watch the video on FolensOnline about Pamela's unplanned teenage pregnancy. Answer the following questions.

1. How did Pamela feel about her pregnancy?

   _____

   _____

2. Why did Pamela get pregnant?

   _____

   _____

3. How did having her son affect Pamela?

   _____

   _____

Your teacher will assign your group one of the following three tasks.

Task 1: In your copy, devise what you think might be a daily schedule for looking after a two-month-old baby. Start from the time the child wakes up until the child goes to sleep at night. If you have a younger sibling or have babysitting experience, share what you know with your group. Include nappy changing, dressing, washing, playing, feeding and naps in your schedule.

Task 2: In your copy, devise what you think might be a daily schedule for looking after a seven-year-old child. Start from the time the child wakes up until the child goes to sleep at night. If you have a younger sibling or have babysitting experience, share what you know with your group. Include feeding, washing, playing, school drop-offs and collections, after-school activities and homework in your schedule.

Task 3: In your copy, devise what you think is a typical Saturday schedule for a teenager. Start from the time the teenager wakes up until the teenager goes to sleep at night. Include socialising, hobbies, eating and activities in your schedule.

Finding help

If you or someone you know is a teen parent or has a crisis pregnancy, you can find information and advice on the Teen Parents Support Programme and HSE Crisis Pregnancy Programme websites.

Write a positive message to a teenager who has a friend who is a teenage mother. He is worried that she is finding it hard and is lonely, but he doesn't know how to help, as he doesn't know anything about babies.

_____

_____

_____

Rapid recap

Topics we discussed today:

1. _____

2. _____

3. _____

3

People or places I could find out more information on this lesson from:

1. _____

2. _____

2

Something in today's lesson that I would like to learn more about:

1. _____

1

Parent's/guardian's signature _____

(Your teacher will tell you if this should be signed each week.)

Go to the Think Contraception website and watch the video about talking to your GP about contraception. Talk to your parents about this topic. Show them the rapid recap if you like.

Complete your personal learning journal at home.

■ Strand review

In this strand, you learned about:

- Body image
- Respect in relationships
- Setting boundaries in relationships
- Sexual health
- Relationship problems
- Responsibilities of pregnancy and parenting

Look back over the lessons that you completed. In the table below, tick the skills that you think you used or learned.

Managing myself
- I know myself better. ◯
- I made decisions. ◯
- I set goals. ◯
- I achieved goals. ◯
- I thought about what I learned. ◯
- I used technology to learn. ◯

Staying well
- I am healthy and active. ◯
- I am social. ◯
- I feel safe. ◯
- I am spiritual. ◯
- I feel confident. ◯
- I feel positive about what I learned. ◯

Communicating
- I used language. ◯
- I used numbers. ◯
- I listened to my classmates. ◯
- I expressed myself. ◯
- I performed/ presented. ◯
- I had a discussion/ debate. ◯
- I used technology to communicate. ◯

Being literate
- I understand some new words. ◯
- I enjoyed words and language. ◯
- I wrote for different reasons. ◯
- I expressed my ideas clearly. ◯
- I developed my spoken language. ◯
- I read and wrote in different ways. ◯

Being creative
- I used my imagination. ◯
- I thought about things from a different point of view. ◯
- I put ideas into action. ◯
- I learned in a creative way. ◯
- I was creative with digital technology. ◯

Working with others
- I developed relationships. ◯
- I dealt with conflict. ◯
- I co-operated. ◯
- I respected difference. ◯
- I helped make the world a better place. ◯
- I learned with others. ◯
- I worked with others using digital technology. ◯

Managing information and thinking
- I was curious. ◯
- I gathered and analysed information. ◯
- I thought creatively. ◯
- I thought about what I learned. ◯
- I used digital technology to access, manage and share information. ◯

Being numerate
- I expressed ideas mathematically. ◯
- I estimated, predicted and calculated. ◯
- I was interested in problem-solving. ◯
- I saw patterns and trends. ◯
- I gathered and presented data. ◯
- I used digital technology to review and understand numbers. ◯

Now write two skills from the list that you think you should focus on more in the future.

_____

_____

My mental health

This strand focuses on building positive mental health, examining young people's experience of mental ill-health and learning how to support yourself and others in challenging times.

Strand learning outcomes

- Appreciate the importance of talking things over, including recognising the links between thoughts, feelings and behaviour

- Practise some relaxation techniques

- Critique mental health services available to young people locally

- Explain the significance of substance use for your mental health

- Practise a range of strategies for building resilience

- Use coping skills for managing life's challenges

- Outline the personal, social, emotional and physical responses to loss and bereavement

- Compare how loss and bereavement are portrayed in a variety of contexts and cultures

- Describe how you might care for yourself and be supportive of others in times of loss or bereavement

20. Dealing with challenges – sleep and diet

At the end of this lesson, you will:

 Understand the role sleep plays in maintaining good mental health and how mental ill-health can affect sleep

 Know how to achieve good-quality sleep

 Appreciate the role of diet in maintaining good mental health

 Key words

abc

Insomnia

Aware
Resilient

Have a quick Pictionary game with the person beside you. Take turns to draw the following and the other person must guess what it is. See who can get all five done the quickest.

- An animal
- A vehicle
- A feeling
- A country
- A school subject

Dealing with challenges

This year you may find that you are facing additional challenges. For example, as you prepare to complete your first state exams, you may experience stress or worry. At times like this, it is important that you take good care of your mental health.

You have already learned about a variety of coping skills in SPHE and the benefits of positive thinking. In this lesson, you will learn about the importance of sleep and diet in maintaining your mental health. In the next lesson, you will learn how relaxation can also help you to deal with these challenges.

Sleep

In times of stress or worry, some people may have difficulty sleeping. When some people are stressed, they may choose to forego sleep or stay up late to get extra work or study done.

You can't function effectively without sleep. You need a good night's sleep to help repair and replace body cells and to maintain your mental health. An occasional night with poor sleep is not going to damage your health, but ongoing insomnia or poor sleep can lead to tiredness, irritability and difficulty concentrating and can affect your mental health.

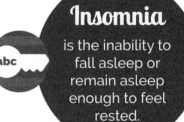

Insomnia is the inability to fall asleep or remain asleep enough to feel rested.

In pairs, list some events or times in a teenager's life when you may be more stressed or worried than usual.

_____

_____

Tips to help develop a good sleep routine

* **Don't take naps.** If possible, avoid taking naps during the day. If you are tired earlier in the day, have a small walk and a snack to give you energy. Does anyone have any other tips for helping you feel refreshed if you are tired in the afternoon?

* **Avoid stimulants.** Food and drinks high in caffeine or sugar can keep you awake, so avoid these, especially in the evening. What are some foods and drinks that are high in caffeine or sugar?

* **Take time to be active.** Exercise (outside if possible), but try to avoid exercise an hour before bedtime, as it may take some time for you to wind down from the exercise.

* **Relax.** Try to relax with deep breathing exercises or progressive muscle relaxation when in bed. Suicide or Survive offer a free 'Softly to Sleep' 13-minute meditation track that you can download from their website. Does anyone use or know any other relaxation exercises that can help you sleep?

 **Lesson 21**

* **Use lavender.** The smell of lavender helps with relaxation – try sprinkling a few drops of lavender oil on your pillow (you can get this in health shops). Are there any other smells that can help you to relax?

* **Wind down.** Have a bedtime routine and wind-down time before going to bed. Turn off all technology and do something restful, such as taking a warm bath or reading a book. Does anyone have any other wind-down activities they like to do before going to bed?

Try the #ZZZ challenge. This 14-day sleep challenge is designed to help you improve your sleep. You can find the #ZZZ challenge on the Your Mental Health website.

It is recommended that teenagers get around 9 hours of sleep every night. Some need more and some need less, but studies show that most teenagers need 9¼ hours of sleep per night.

1. Work out the average amount of sleep that the students in your group get on a school night.

   _____

2. Work out the average amount of sleep that the students in your group get on a non-school night.

   _____

3. How many students in your group use their phone in bed last thing at night? (If so, for how long?)

   _____

4. How many students in your group use their phone in bed first thing in the morning? (If so, for how long?)

   _____

How sleep can affect mental health

Not sleeping well over a long period of time can cause mental ill-health or it may make existing mental health illnesses worse. Here are some ways that sleep can affect your mental health:

* If you are constantly tired you might skip social outings, so you might see less of your friends or family. Being isolated or lonely can lead to mental health problems.

* Being tired makes it harder to cope and think clearly. Everyday challenges become much more difficult when you are tired.

* Lack of sleep can affect your mood and energy levels. Being in bad form can cause you to think more negatively, which can also affect your mental health.

List some common emotions felt when you are really tired or have had very little sleep.

_____

_____

_____

▆ Food for good mental health ▆

 Lesson 6

Eating well can improve your mental health and help you deal with the challenges you may face. Your brain needs nutrients, just like your heart, lungs and muscles do. This year, because you are busy studying and may be under pressure or stressed, it is more important than ever to eat well. The following foods have extra benefits that help the brain to function well, so try to include them in your daily diet.

* **Wholegrain cereals:** These release glucose (sugar) slowly into the bloodstream, keeping you mentally alert throughout the day. Opt for brown or wholegrain cereals, such as whole wheat pasta, brown bread, granary bread, multigrain bread, wholegrain rice and oats.

* **Omega-3s:** This is a fatty acid that can't be made by the body. Omega-3s help you to manage stress and improve memory. It also helps make serotonin, the good mood brain chemical. The best sources of omega-3s are oily fish such as salmon, tuna or mackerel. Plant sources include walnuts, pumpkin seeds and soya beans.

* **Colourful fruit and vegetables:** Eating a variety of colourful fruit and vegetables, such as blackcurrants, blueberries, broccoli, carrots, kiwis, oranges and tomatoes, makes sure that you get an excellent source of a variety of vitamins to keep your brain and memory sharp.

In groups, plan a daily menu for a teenager (breakfast, lunch, dinner and snacks) that is rich in the nutrients and foods mentioned on the previous page.

MENU

Write a positive message to a teenager who constantly sleeps poorly due to nightmares but doesn't want to say it to anyone in case they think she is being childish.

_____

_____

_____

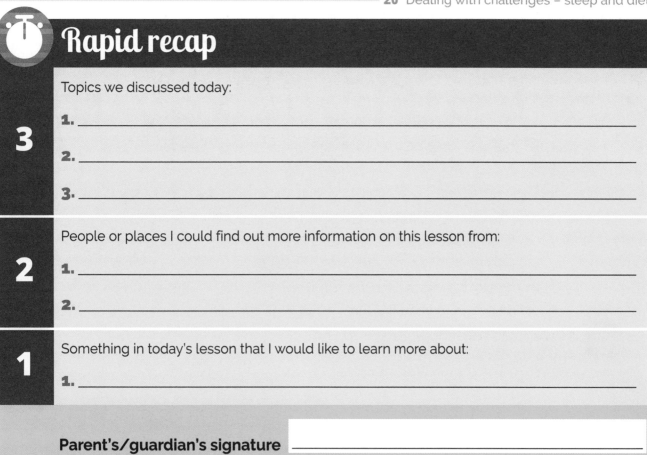

Rapid recap

3

Topics we discussed today:

1. _____

2. _____

3. _____

2

People or places I could find out more information on this lesson from:

1. _____

2. _____

1

Something in today's lesson that I would like to learn more about:

1. _____

Parent's/guardian's signature _____

(Your teacher will tell you if this should be signed each week.)

Go to the ReachOut website and find more advice on improving sleep quality and dealing with insomnia (look up 'Sleeping problems' on the site's search engine). Write some suggestions below.

_____

_____

_____

Complete your personal learning journal at home.

21. Dealing with challenges – relaxation

At the end of this lesson, you will:

 Have examined how you relax

 Understand the importance of relaxation

 Know how to initiate the relaxation response

 Have practised progressive muscle relaxation

 Key words abc

Relaxation response

Progressive muscle relaxation

Aware

Resilient

Your teacher will put up an Agree sign and a Disagree sign on different sides of the classroom. Stand at the right place in the classroom according to whether you agree or disagree with the following statements.

- Stress is bad for you.
- Physical health is more important than mental health.
- Watching TV is the best way to relax.
- Playing sport helps me to relax.
- Teenagers don't have time to relax.

Relaxation

Relaxation is an excellent way to deal with the challenges you might face and the stress that you may feel. Often when we want to relax we watch TV or catch up on social media on our phone, but this does little to reduce the damaging effects of stress. In fact, having so many social media accounts or apps that notify you and that you have to reply to can be stressful in itself!

To effectively reduce stress, you need to activate the body's natural relaxation response. You can do this by practising relaxation techniques such as deep breathing, meditation, rhythmic exercise and yoga. Fitting these activities into your life can help reduce everyday stress, boost your energy and mood, and improve your mental and physical health.

Discuss the stresses brought on by using social media and various apps to communicate with others. How do you feel if you can't access these? Do you ever feel stressed that you have so many things to respond to? Do you ever get stressed if people don't reply to you or comment on your posts or photos?

In pairs, make a list of rules or guidelines for teenagers regarding social media or phone usage that will ensure that teenagers spend less time on social media and more time on exercise or relaxation.

_____

_____

_____

_____

_____

The relaxation response

When you get very stressed, your body is flooded with chemicals that prepare you for 'fight or flight'. This stress response can be lifesaving in emergency situations where you need to act quickly, but when it's constantly activated by the stresses of everyday life, it can wear your body down and take a toll on your mental health.

No one can avoid all stress. A certain amount of stress can be healthy and motivate you to work well. However, you can reduce the effects of stress by learning how to activate the body's relaxation response, a state of deep rest that is the opposite of the stress response.

When the relaxation response is activated:

* Your heart rate slows down.

* Your breathing becomes slower and deeper.

* Your muscles relax.

* Blood flow to the brain increases.

In addition, activating the relaxation response over time may increase your energy and focus, help prevent illness, increase problem-solving abilities, and boost motivation and productivity.

How to produce the relaxation response

There is no single relaxation technique that is best for everyone. The right relaxation technique is the one that works for you and fits your lifestyle. Try some of the following.

Deep breathing

With its focus on full, cleansing breaths, deep breathing is a simple yet powerful relaxation technique. You learned two different deep breathing exercises in First Year and Second Year. Can you remember these?

My Life 1, Lesson 21

My Life 2, Lesson 24

Progressive muscle relaxation

Another way to relax is by using progressive muscle relaxation. This is a two-step process in which you tense and relax different muscle groups in the body. As your body relaxes, so will your mind.

Start at your feet and work your way up to your face, trying to only tense those muscles intended.

* Loosen your clothing, take off your shoes and get comfortable.

* Take a few minutes to breathe in and out in slow, deep breaths.

* When you're ready, shift your attention to your right foot. Take a moment to focus on the way it feels.

* Slowly tense the muscles in your right foot, squeezing as tightly as you can. Hold for a count of 10.

* Relax your foot. Focus on the tension flowing away and how your foot feels as the tension leaves your body.

* Stay in this relaxed state for a moment, breathing deeply and slowly.

* Now focus on your left foot. Squeeze for 10 seconds and release, feeling your foot go loose and all the tension evaporating.

* Move slowly up through your body, contracting and relaxing the different muscle groups.

Progressive muscle relaxation sequence:

* Right foot, then left foot
* Right calf, then left calf
* Right thigh, then left thigh
* Hips and buttocks
* Stomach

* Chest
* Back
* Right arm and hand, then left arm and hand
* Neck and shoulders
* Face

Practise progressive muscle relaxation as a class. Turn off the lights, make yourself comfortable and listen to a guided progressive muscle relaxation video on YouTube.

Rhythmic exercise

The idea of exercising may not sound particularly soothing or relaxing, but certain exercises that get you into a flow of repetitive or rhythmic movement can be very relaxing and will release hormones that make you feel better.

Examples of rhythmic exercise that can be relaxing include:

* Running
* Dancing
* Rowing
* Swimming
* Walking

To make the most of rhythmic exercise, you should try to be mindful. Being mindful means being fully engaged and paying attention to how your body feels at that time rather than thinking about your daily worries or concerns. In order to 'turn off' your thoughts, focus on your breathing and the feelings in your limbs.

 Write a positive message to a Third Year student who finds it difficult to relax after school because he has so much homework to do, but he also finds it hard to relax after doing homework because he is so tired.

_____

_____

_____

_____

Rapid recap

3

Topics we discussed today:

1. _____
2. _____
3. _____

2

People or places I could find out more information on this lesson from:

1. _____
2. _____

1

Something in today's lesson that I would like to learn more about:

1. _____

Parent's/guardian's signature _____

(Your teacher will tell you if this should be signed each week.)

1. Write down two exercises or activities that you do that initiate the relaxation response.

   _____
   _____

2. How often do you do this?

   _____

3. Aim to try one relaxation exercise and one rhythmic exercise this week.

Complete your personal learning journal at home.

22. Coping with loss

At the end of this lesson, you will:

 Have identified the feelings associated with grief

 Have developed your language skills for discussing death

 Have an understanding of the grieving process

 Know where to get help and how to help a friend who is grieving

 Key words abc

Bereavement

Grief

🧠 Aware
🤲 Connected
🌱 Resilient

In Second Year you learned about the feeling of loss, in particular the loss felt when a family or parents separate. This lesson focuses on the loss felt when someone dies, which is called grief. It could be the death of a family member, a family pet or a friend. Sometimes we can even experience a sense of loss when a person dies who is not even very close to us, for example if someone in your school community dies. The way you grieve can be influenced by how old you are, the way a person died and how close you were to that person.

My Life 2, Lesson 22

Think about a really happy day that you shared with a loved one. What was the weather like? What colours, tastes, textures and smells remind you of that day? Make a simple bookmark and decorate it with these thoughts and memories.

Grief is the loss felt when someone dies.

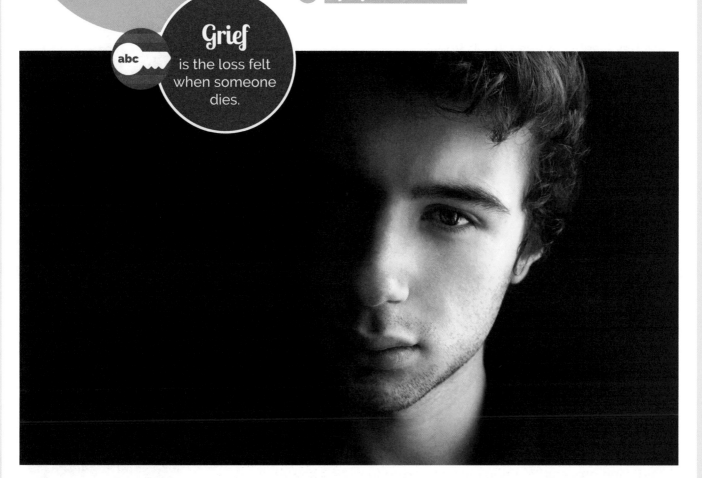

Stages of grief

No matter how someone died, it is never easy to face. You may have heard of the grieving process. This is a healing process you go through after a loved one dies. There are five well-known stages of grief, first written about by a woman named Elisabeth Kübler-Ross.

The stages are:

* **Denial:** You refuse to believe that the person has died. You think, 'This isn't happening to me.'

* **Anger:** You are angry with the person for dying or angry that you have to deal with it. You are angry that this is happening to you.

* **Bargaining:** You try to make deals and look for a way out by saying things such as, 'If I did this, then...'

* **Depression:** You don't seem to care about anything any more. You think, 'What's the point?' or 'Why bother?'

* **Acceptance:** You realise that your life will go on, but this does not mean that the pain and sense of loss will go away.

It is important to understand that:

* These stages are not meant to be complete or necessarily happen in this order.

* Not everyone will feel all these feelings, because reactions to death are unique. There is no right or wrong way to grieve.

* There is no set timetable for grieving. Nobody can say exactly when it will start or end.

 Discuss how the way that a person died might influence your grief.

Coping with bereavement

There are practical things you can do to get through a time of bereavement or loss.

* **Talk.** Talking is often a good way to soothe painful emotions. Talking to a friend, family member or counsellor can help with the healing process.

* **Allow yourself to feel sad and to cry.** It's a healthy part of the grieving process. You don't have to pretend to be okay when you are not.

* **Keep your routine.** Keeping up simple things like walking the dog or playing football can help.

* **Sleep.** Emotional upset can make you very tired, so you might need to sleep more than usual.

* **Avoid things that numb the pain, such as alcohol.** It will only make you feel worse once the numbness wears off.

* **Go to counselling if it feels right for you.** Counselling may be more useful after a couple of weeks or months. Only you will know when you are ready. Look for Rainbows groups in your school or area on the Rainbows Ireland website or talk to your school guidance counsellor.

abc **Bereavement**
A state of loss after a loved one has died.

Remembering the person who has died

There are many ways to remember the person who has died. People particularly like to mark the occasion of the anniversary of the person's death or their birthday. Here are some other examples:

* Look at photos of them together with friends or family and talk about the day they were taken.

* Plant a tree in their memory and think of them when you see it growing.

* Get together with family or friends on their birthday. Maybe release a sky lantern or some balloons.

* Pray for them.

* Talk to them in your head or write to them in your diary.

* Have a memory jar. Every time you think about them, write it on a piece of paper and put it in a jar, even simple things like her favourite colour was yellow or he hated tomato ketchup. These little things may mean a lot to you as your memories fade over time.

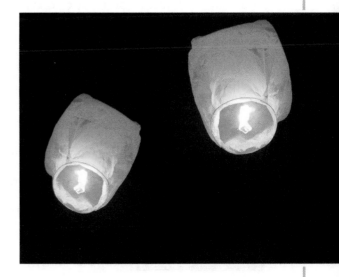

Does anyone have any other suggestions on how to mark the anniversary of a loved one's death or birthday? Discuss a film or TV programme in which someone dies. How do the bereaved grieve or react to the death?

The following words are associated with death and grief. In groups, find out what they mean by using a dictionary or an online dictionary, then explain them in your own words.

Bereavement: _____

The bereaved: _____

Deceased: _____

Mourning: _____

Sympathies/condolences: _____

Wake: _____

Mass card: _____

■ Helping a bereaved friend ■

It can be hard to know what to say or do when someone you care about is grieving. You may feel helpless, awkward or unsure. You may be afraid of intruding, saying the wrong thing or making the person feel even worse. Or maybe you feel there is little you can do to make things better.

While you can't take away the pain of the loss, you can provide much-needed comfort and support. There are many ways to help a grieving friend or family member. You can do this in the following ways:

* **Acknowledge the death.** Example: 'I heard that your _____ died.'

* **Express your sympathy.** Example: 'I'm sorry to hear that.'

* **Be honest.** Example: 'I'm not sure what to say or do, but I want you to know I'm here for you.'

* **Offer your support.** Example: 'Tell me what I can do for you.'

* **Ask how he or she feels.** Don't assume that you know how he or she feels.

* **Listen.** Try simply asking: 'Do you feel like talking about it?'

Barnardos and Rainbows Ireland have excellent advice for dealing with loss on their websites.

Write a positive message to Oisín, who feels sad that he forgets lots of things about his cousin whom he was very close to before she died two years ago. He is feeling guilty that he doesn't think of her every day now.

_____

_____

_____

Rapid recap

3

Topics we discussed today:

1. _____

2. _____

3. _____

2

People or places I could find out more information on this lesson from:

1. _____

2. _____

1

Something in today's lesson that I would like to learn more about:

1. _____

Parent's/guardian's signature _____

(Your teacher will tell you if this should be signed each week.)

In your personal learning journal, write about a happy time that you shared with a loved one who has died.

Complete your personal learning journal at home.

23. Substance use and mental health

At the end of this lesson, you will:

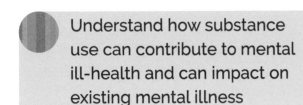 Understand how substance use can contribute to mental ill-health and can impact on existing mental illness

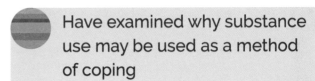 Have examined why substance use may be used as a method of coping

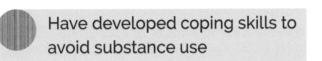 Have developed coping skills to avoid substance use

Key words
abc
Substance use

Aware
Resilient

Your group must come up with five points for the school debate team on the following motion: 'The legal age for drinking alcohol in Ireland should be lowered to 16.' Your teacher will tell you if your group is for or against the motion.

Substance use

As you learned in the last few lessons, eating a balanced diet, sleeping well, relaxing and talking about problems with friends or a counsellor are all healthy ways to deal with stress, cope with loss and deal with challenges.

An unhealthy approach to dealing with such challenges is substance use. People may turn to drugs and/or alcohol because they can affect the way they feel and think. The effect that drugs and alcohol have on a person will depend on the individual's mental and physical state as well as their mood. It will also depend on the quantity and mix of substances used.

abc Substance use is the harmful use of alcohol or drugs.

Lesson 11, 12 and 13

Do you think that movies and television make alcohol or drug use look attractive or unattractive? Does that influence teenagers' decisions about alcohol and drugs?

Impact of substance use on mental health

* The negative effects of some substances are similar to the symptoms of some mental illnesses. For example, people who use cannabis can experience paranoia, anxiety and panic attacks.

* People may use substances as a way to cope with a mental illness instead of being properly diagnosed and using the correct medication.

* Drugs such as cannabis, alcohol, ecstasy and heroin affect a user's mood. They can arouse certain emotions or dull other feelings. These changes in mood or behaviour are the result of changes to the brain, which can cause mental ill-health.

* Taking too much of a drug or a certain mix of substances can permanently disrupt the chemical balance in your brain.

* Serotonin is a chemical naturally found in the brain. It is sometimes referred to as the 'happy hormone'. Drugs such as ecstasy cause the brain to release extra serotonin. Over time, serotonin stores decrease so much that depression can occur.

* Schizophrenia is a severe mental illness that may cause you to hear voices in your head and believe that other people are trying to control or harm you. Research shows a link between cannabis use and schizophrenia. The risk is also greater in younger people who use cannabis and those who smoke it regularly.

* Alcohol is a depressant, which means it can disrupt the balance of chemicals and processes in the brain, affecting thoughts, feelings and actions. This can lead to anger, aggression, anxiousness and depression.

Go to the Alcohol Action Ireland website and find out more about alcohol and mental health. Write down three things that you find out below.

_____

_____

_____

Dylan hasn't had an easy home life. Now he is having a very hard time at school too. His older brother left school last year and spends most days at home smoking weed or in the park drinking with his friends at the weekends. Dylan doesn't want that to be his life, but it would be easy for him to do and would help him forget his problems.

Imagine you are Dylan's friend and he asks you for advice. Help him to come up with a plan in order to avoid using alcohol or drugs as a way of dealing with challenges. In your group, think about the following and fill in the table.

Places he can go to avoid alcohol/drugs	People he can talk to	Activities he can do	Things he can say if his brother or others try to persuade him to drink or use drugs

Imagine that some day you will have children. In your copy, write an email with advice for them to read when they are 16. Tell them what you think about alcohol and drugs and how you hope they will deal with challenges in their lives.

Write a positive message to Clodagh, who is experiencing a lot of stress at the moment and finds that the best way to forget about her problems is by getting drunk.

_____

_____

_____

_____

⏱ Rapid recap

3

Topics we discussed today:

1. _____

2. _____

3. _____

2

People or places I could find out more information on this lesson from:

1. _____

2. _____

1

Something in today's lesson that I would like to learn more about:

1. _____

Parent's/guardian's signature _____

(Your teacher will tell you if this should be signed each week.)

Go to the Drugs.ie website and find out more about the Let's Talk About Drugs National Youth Media Awards. Watch the videos from the winning entries from previous years.

Complete your personal learning journal at home.

24. Minding my mental health

At the end of this lesson, you will:

 Have reflected on your own mental health

 Know how to help yourself and others if you experience mental ill-health

Key words
abc Self-esteem

 Aware
 Connected
 Resilient

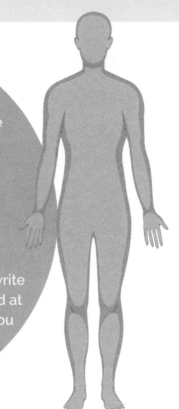

Next to the body, write one positive thing that you are thankful for in relation to each of the following body parts:

Your head

Your hands

Your feet

Your heart

For example, for your head, you could write something along the lines of 'I am good at remembering stuff'. For your hands, you could write something like 'I have neat handwriting.'

Positive thinking

Thinking positively can help you to solve problems, achieve your goals, improve your self-esteem and improve your mental health. If you can learn to think positively all or most of the time, it can have a positive effect on how you feel and behave.

In order to help you think positively:

* **Try to think of a positive thought every time you have a negative thought.** For example, if you think 'I'll never be as smart as him', try thinking, 'I may not be as smart as him, but I am a good footballer.'

* **Talk positively about yourself – don't put yourself down.** This doesn't mean being boastful, just recognising your own strengths and being happy with who you are.

* **Talk positively about others.** Respect for others and from others can help you to become more confident.

Self-esteem

How one regards or sees themselves.

Think Positive

Student self-reflection

Throughout this year and over the last two years in SPHE, you have learned about positive thinking, recognising stress, dealing with stress and frustration, expressing yourself, positive self-esteem, eating well and exercise. All these topics and many more are important to your mental health and your overall wellbeing.

Reflect on what you have learned about mental health, then answer the following questions (your answers are private).

1. Three things I am doing well to support or improve my mental health:

   _____

   _____

   _____

2. Three things I plan to do that will help to support or improve my mental health:

   _____

   _____

   _____

3. Who would you talk to if you thought you had a mental illness?

   _____

4. What would you do if you found out your friend had been diagnosed with a mental illness?

   _____

   _____

On a piece of paper, draw a flower like the one shown here and cut it out. On each petal and in the centre of the flower, write the following:

- Something positive about yourself
- Something positive that you have achieved
- One thing that makes you feel good about yourself
- One person who makes you feel good about yourself
- Something positive that you would like to achieve
- A compliment you received in the past that has made you feel good

Working in groups, make a list of mental health services that are available in your area, in your community or in your school, such as awareness groups, support groups and medical services. Discuss the following:

- Are these services well advertised?
- Are they easy to access?
- Are there many mental health services to support young people in your area?

You may consider working with one of these mental health services next year if you are doing community action work in Transition Year or you could plan to raise awareness of one of these services as part of a TY project.

Write a positive message to Maeve, who is trying to exercise and think positively because she knows that they are important for her mental health, but old habits are creeping back in and she is finding it very hard.

_____
_____
_____
_____
_____
_____
_____
_____
_____

Rapid recap

3

Topics we discussed today:

1. _____

2. _____

3. _____

2

People or places I could find out more information on this lesson from:

1. _____

2. _____

1

Something in today's lesson that I would like to learn more about:

1. _____

Parent's/guardian's signature _____

(Your teacher will tell you if this should be signed each week.)

Strand review

In this strand, you learned about:

- Dealing with challenges – sleep and diet
- Dealing with challenges – relaxation
- Coping with loss
- Substance use and mental health
- Minding your mental health

Look back over the lessons that you completed. In the table below, tick the skills that you think you learned or used.

Managing myself
- I know myself better. ○
- I made decisions. ○
- I set goals. ○
- I achieved goals. ○
- I thought about what I learned. ○
- I used technology to learn. ○

Staying well
- I am healthy and active. ○
- I am social. ○
- I feel safe. ○
- I am spiritual. ○
- I feel confident. ○
- I feel positive about what I learned. ○

Communicating
- I used language. ○
- I used numbers. ○
- I listened to my classmates. ○
- I expressed myself. ○
- I performed/ presented. ○
- I had a discussion/ debate. ○
- I used technology to communicate. ○

Being literate
- I understand some new words. ○
- I enjoyed words and language. ○
- I wrote for different reasons. ○
- I expressed my ideas clearly. ○
- I developed my spoken language. ○
- I read and wrote in different ways. ○

Being creative
- I used my imagination. ○
- I thought about things from a different point of view. ○
- I put ideas into action. ○
- I learned in a creative way. ○
- I was creative with digital technology. ○

Working with others
- I developed relationships. ○
- I dealt with conflict. ○
- I co-operated. ○
- I respected difference. ○
- I helped make the world a better place. ○
- I learned with others. ○
- I worked with others using digital technology. ○

Managing information and thinking
- I was curious. ○
- I gathered and analysed information. ○
- I thought creatively. ○
- I thought about what I learned. ○
- I used digital technology to access, manage and share information. ○

Being numerate
- I expressed ideas mathematically. ○
- I estimated, predicted and calculated. ○
- I was interested in problem-solving. ○
- I saw patterns and trends. ○
- I gathered and presented data. ○
- I used digital technology to review and understand numbers. ○

Now write two skills from the list that you think you should focus on more in the future.

_____

_____

Glossary

A

Abstinence: Choosing not to have sexual intercourse.

Age of consent: The age at which a person is considered legally able to consent to sexual activity.

Aggressive communication: A tendency to attack or be hostile to others.

Ailment: A complaint or illness.

Assertive communication: Confident and clear in stating your point.

B

Bereavement: A state of loss after a loved one has died.

Binge drinking: The practice of drinking large amounts of alcohol at one time with the aim of getting drunk.

Body image: Your view of how you see yourself.

Boundary: A limit or line you don't want to cross.

Bystander: A person who sees bullying happening.

C

Caesarean section: A surgical procedure to deliver a baby.

Communicate: The way to convey feelings or thoughts to others.

Community: A large group of people who have something in common.

Conception: The action of conceiving or creating a child.

Conflict: A disagreement or difference between people.

Consequence: Something that happens as a result of a decision or action.

Constructive criticism: Advice or feedback that is useful and intended to be helpful or improve something.

Contraception: A method or device used to prevent pregnancy.

Contract: A document that records an agreement.

Conventional: A socially accepted style or idea.

Criticism: An expression of disapproval of someone or something.

Cyber: Relating to the internet or computers.

D

Desirable: Something good or pleasing that you would like to have.

Divorce: A legal ending of a marriage.

Drug: A chemical substance that alters the body or mind.

E

Embryo: A fertilised egg from conception to eight weeks.

Emotion: A strong feeling about something or someone.

F

Fatal: Causing death.

Fertility: The ability to have children.

Foetus: The term for an unborn human baby from eight weeks after conception.

Frustration: A feeling of disappointment, exasperation or weakness caused by goals not being met or desires being unsatisfied.

G

Gender identity: Describes how a person feels about their own gender.

Goal: Something that you aim to achieve.

Grief: The loss felt when someone dies.

H

Hereditary: Passed on through your family.

Heterosexual: The term for people who are attracted to members of the opposite sex.

Homosexual: The term for people who are attracted to members of the same sex.

I

Identity theft: A crime where someone steals your personal information and uses it to their advantage.

Independent: Capable of thinking and acting without consulting others.

Influence: To affect someone's thinking or actions.

Inhibition: A feeling that makes you self-conscious and more reserved.

Insomnia: The inability to fall asleep or remain asleep enough to feel rested.

Interpersonal skills: The skills used to communicate and interact with other people, both individually and in groups.

L

Loss: A feeling of sadness, loneliness or emptiness at the absence of something or someone.

M

Maturity: The full development of something or someone.

Mental health: Includes your emotional, psychological and social wellbeing.

Motivation: What drives or inspires you to do something.

N

Nutritional label: A label found on most packaged foods that shows the amount of each nutrient in a set amount of the food, e.g. 100 grams.

O

Obstacle: Something that may prevent you from achieving your goal.

P

Passive communication: Tending to avoid expressing your opinions or feelings.

Passive smoking: Inhaling someone else's cigarette smoke.

Physical effect: A change in the body.

Psychological effect: A change in the mind.

R

Relationship: A link or bond that you have with another person.

Responsibility: A duty attached to your role.

Right: Something that you are entitled to.

Role: The position you occupy in a group, e.g. your role in the family.

S

Self-esteem: How one regards or sees themselves.

Separation: The act of stopping living together as a couple.

Sexting: Sharing sexual texts, videos or photographic content (nude photos) using phones, apps, social networks and other technologies.

STI: This stands for sexually transmitted infection, which is an infection that is passed on from an infected partner through sexual activity.

Substance use: The harmful use of alcohol or drugs.

Symptom: A sign or indication of a medical condition.

V

Virgin: Someone who has never had sexual intercourse.

Help agencies

Abuse

Amen

This site provides support for male victims of domestic abuse. It also offers help to their children.

www.amen.ie

Childline

Childline gives support to young people through a freephone 24-hour listening service and through its website. All calls are free of charge and confidential. You can chat live on the website or if you have been affected by bullying you can text the word 'Bully' to 50101. These services are available from 10am to 4am every day.

Freephone helpline: 1800 666 666

You can also contact Teentext by texting 'Talk' to 50101 (this is an automated free text support service)

www.childline.ie

TeenLine

TeenLine Ireland is a confidential helpline service for teenagers to help them deal with any problems or worries they are experiencing.

Freephone helpline: 1800 833 634

www.teenline.ie

Women's Aid

Women's Aid helps women and children who are suffering physical, mental/emotional and/or sexual abuse in their homes.

Freephone helpline: 1800 341 900

www.womensaid.ie

Addiction

Alateen

Alateen is for young people aged 12 to 20 who are affected by a problem drinker either at home or in their circle.

Email: info@al-anon-ireland.org

Tel: 01 873 2699

www.al-anon-ireland.org

Alcoholics Anonymous

Alcoholics Anonymous is a fellowship of men and women who share their experiences, strength and hope with each other in order to solve their common problem and help others to recover from alcoholism.

Email: gso@alcoholicsanonymous.ie

Tel: 01 453 8998

www.alcoholicsanonymous.ie

drugs.ie

This website provides information, support and counselling in relation to drugs, substance misuse or addiction.

Tel: 01 836 0911

www.drugs.ie

Narcotics Anonymous

Narcotics Anonymous is a group of recovering addicts who have found a way to live without the use of drugs. It costs nothing to be a member; the only thing needed is a desire to stop using drugs.

Email: info@na-ireland.org

www.na-ireland.org

National drugs and HIV helpline

This helpline gives confidential support and information for drug users and those affected by HIV.

Freephone helpline: 1800 459 459

■ Bereavement and separation

Barnardos Bereavement Counselling for Children

Barnardos Bereavement Counselling for Children is a service for children and young people run by the Barnardos charity.

Dublin tel: 01 453 0355

Dublin email: bereavement@barnardos.ie

Cork tel: 021 431 0591

Cork email: bereavement@cork.barnardos.ie

www.barnardos.ie

Barnardos Bereavement Helpline

Tel: 01 473 2110 (Monday–Friday, 10am–12 noon)

Bereavement Counselling Service

Administration Office, Dublin Street, Baldoyle, Dublin 13

Tel: 01 839 1766

Rainbows Ireland

The Rainbows 'spectrum programme' is a service that runs support group programmes for young people who have experienced loss due to bereavement or separation/divorce. The programme is specifically for 12- to 18-year-olds.

www.rainbowsireland.com

Teen Between

Teen Between is a support service especially for teenagers whose parents are going through a divorce or separation.

Freephone: 1800 303 191

Email: teenbetween@mrcs.ie

www.teenbetween.ie

■ Body image

Bodywhys

Bodywhys offers support, information and understanding for people with eating disorders.

www.bodywhys.ie

■ Bullying

ReachOut

This website offers information and advice on what to do if you are being bullied.

www.reachout.com

Stop the Bully

Stop the Bully Ireland is an anti-bullying service that empowers people at all ages with the tools to effectively deal with bullying.

www.stopthebully.ie

■ Exams and careers

Qualifax

This website gives information on further and higher education and training courses. It also has tips for studying.

www.qualifax.ie

School Days

This is a resource for parents, teachers and students, including study advice.

www.schooldays.ie

Health

Get Ireland Active

Tools, advice and resources for getting active and a link to the Get Ireland Active app.

www.getirelandactive.ie

Irish Cancer Society

This site gives information and support to those who have been diagnosed with cancer or who are affected by someone they know having cancer.

Freephone: 1800 200 700

www.cancer.ie

Irish Heart Foundation

The Irish Heart Foundation supports those managing heart disease and strokes.

LoCall: 1890 432 787

www.irishheart.ie

Safefood

This website provides food safety, healthy eating and food hygiene advice for consumers along with healthy recipes and guidelines.

www.safefood.eu

Mental health and depression

Aware

Aware is an organisation that provides information and emotional support to people who experience depression as well as their families.

www.aware.ie

Grow

Grow helps people who have suffered, or are suffering, from mental health problems.

www.grow.ie

HeadsUp

HeadsUp is a 24-hour text support and information service provided by Rehab. Text the word 'Headsup' to 50424. A list of topics will be sent to you. Choose a topic and you will instantly be sent a list of confidential helpline numbers, including where to go for help in a crisis.

www.headsup.ie

Jigsaw

Jigsaw supports young people with their mental health and wellbeing. Jigsaw is a community-based service linked to Headstrong.

www.jigsaw.ie

Mental Health Ireland

This is a national voluntary organisation that aims to promote mental health and to support people with a mental illness.

www.mentalhealthireland.ie

Mindfulness Centre

This website has information on mindfulness, courses and retreats as well as excellent resources to help you practise mindfulness at home.

www.mindfulness.ie

National Office for Suicide Prevention

The National Office for Suicide Prevention provides information about support services in your area.

www.nosp.ie

Pieta House

Pieta House is a centre that offers help to people thinking about suicide or self-harm.

www.pieta.ie

ReachOut

ReachOut provides mental health information and includes inspiring real-life stories from young people to help other young people get through tough times.

www.reachout.ie

Samaritans

The Samaritans is a 24-hour confidential support service for anyone who is experiencing feelings of distress or despair, including those who have thoughts of suicide, and want someone to talk to.

Callsave: 1850 609 090

www.samaritans.org

St Patrick's Mental Health Services

Website of Ireland's largest independent not-for-profit mental health service and hospital.

www.stpatricks.ie

yourmentalhealth.ie

This website provides general information and advice on looking after your mental health.

www.yourmentalhealth.ie

Pregnancy

Irish Family Planning Agency

The Irish Family Planning Agency provides information, advice and support to young people on sex, sexual health, relationships and pregnancy.

www.ifpa.ie

Sexuality, relationships and sexual health

Barnardos

Advice to teenagers on friendship and relationship problems.

www.barnardos.ie

BeLonG To

BeLonG To runs youth groups for lesbian, gay, bisexual and transgender (LGBT) young people aged 14 to 18. They also have a forum on their website.

www.belongto.org

Spunout

Spunout is a web-based initiative for young people aged 17 to 24. It provides young people with access to information, support and resources to lead happy, healthy and fulfilled lives.

www.spunout.ie

TeensHealth

Facts and advice on nutrition, moods, sex, infections, body image and relationships.

www.teenshealth.org

Violence

2in2u.ie

This quiz is designed to help you figure out if you are in an unhealthy relationship.

www.2in2u.ie

CARI

CARI provides a confidential helpline service for anyone with concerns about the sexual abuse of a child or young person. CARI also provides a counselling service.

LoCall helpline: 1890 924 567

Email: helpline@cari.ie

www.cari.ie

Childline

Contact Childline for information and support.

Freephone helpline: 1800 666 666

Text support: Text 'List' to 50101 (this is an automated free text support service)

www.childline.ie

HSE

Contact a social worker at your local HSE health centre. For details of services in your area, call the HSE Infoline.

LoCall: 1850 24 1850

www.hse.ie

Women's Aid

Contact the Women's Aid National Freephone Helpline 1800 341 900 for information on your local domestic abuse support service or refuge.

www.womensaid.ie